International Management English

Managing Projects

Bob Dignen

DELTA Publishing
Quince Cottage
Hoe Lane
Peaslake
Surrey GU5 9SW
England

York Associates
Peasholme House
St Saviours Place
York YO1 7PJ
England

www.deltapublishing.co.uk

www.york-associates.co.uk

First published 2012

Edited by Catriona Watson-Brown
Designed by Caroline Johnston
Photos by Shutterstock (pages 8, 10, 12, 18, 22, 24, 28 Aija
Lehtonen/Shutterstock.com, 33, 38, 40, 50, 55, 60 (left), 64, 75
(both), 80); Fotosearch (page 14 © aksakalko/www.fotosearch.com);
Rex Features (page 30); iStock (pages 31, 44, 45, 48, 58, 60 (right),
70, 78, 85)
Cartoon by CartoonStock (page 65)
Cover photo © NASA
Cover design by Clare Webber
Printed in Malta by Melita Press

ISBN 978-1-905085-66-8

Author acknowledgements
The author would like to thank Chris Hartley and Catriona Watson-
Brown for their support during this project.

Text acknowledgements
We are grateful to the following for permission to reproduce copyright
material:
Carl Robinson, Ph.D., Advanced Leadership Consulting for an extract
adapted from *Managing Virtual Teams*, 2006 by Carl Robinson, Ph.D.,
http://www.leadershipconsulting.com. Reproduced by permission;
Cengage Learning, Inc. for extracts and a table from *50 Ways to
improve your Intercultural Skills* by Bob Dignen and James Chamberlain,
pp.15, 63, 2009, copyright © 2010, Heinle/ELT, a part of Cengage
Learning, Inc. Reproduced by permission, www.cengage.com/
permissions; Roffey Park Institute for a table from *Building Global
Leadership: Strategies for Success* by Sinclair, A. and Agyeman, B., 2004,
copyright © Roffey Park Institute; Cambridge University Press for an
extract adapted from 'Creating a team feedback culture' in
Communicating Across Cultures by Bob Dignen, 2010, p.45. Reproduced
by permission from Cambridge University Press; David Swink for an
extract adapted from 'Managing Conflicts with Email: Why It's So
Tempting' by David F. Swink, *Psychology Today*, 14 January 2010,
copyright © David F. Swink; and Dr A.J. Schuler for an extract adapted
from 'Overcoming Resistance to Change: Top Ten Reasons for Change
Resistance' by A. J. Schuler, Psy. D., copyright © 2003 A.J. Schuler,
Psy. D. Dr A.J. Schuler is an expert in leadership and organizational
change. To find out more about his programs and services, visit
www.SchulerSolutions.com or call (703) 370-6545.

In some instances we have been unable to trace the owners of
copyright material and we would appreciate any information that
would enable us to do so.

Contents

Introduction

At York Associates, we always aim to develop the skills which help professionals to do their jobs better. In recent years, we have worked hard to enrich our Business English and professional communication training with intercultural content. More recently, we have included a focus on important interpersonal and management skills for listening, building relationships and trust, influencing, etc.

Our approach is built on the premise that good communication is vital to achieving results at work. Effective international communicators need a blend of language, professional communication, intercultural and management skills to be successful.

Welcome to *International Management English*, a new series published jointly by York Associates and Delta Publishing. The four titles in this series are:
- *Leading People*
- *Managing Projects*
- *Working Virtually*
- *Managing Change*

Each book includes either one or two audio CDs.

Professional language training with a management focus

Each book consists of eight units of study, containing four main sections per unit:
- *Section A: Discussion and listening*
  Engaging and relevant content in areas of international management and teamwork
- *Section B: Communication skills*
  Opportunities for the practice of key skills in areas such as conflict management, team building and giving/receiving feedback, as well as more familiar topics such as presentations, meetings, negotiations and writing e-mails
- *Section C: Professional skills*
  Authentic texts from leading management writers and thinkers, designed to encourage reflection and debate among readers
- *Section D: Intercultural competence and Case study*
  A focus on raising intercultural awareness, followed by illustrative case studies which are drawn from the authors' experience of the international business world

In addition, the book offers:
- a strong emphasis on vocabulary learning, with glossaries of key terms at the end of each unit
- practical tips on how to improve performance at work
- the opportunity to use a learning diary, which encourages the setting of realistic goals to implement the learning points from each unit.

At the end of the book, the Word list provides a useful list of key words, referenced to the page where the term is found.

Having worked through the book, you will have developed not only your business language skills but also your ability to communicate and manage real challenges in your international working environment.

To the teacher

The four titles in this series represent a new development in ELT. They broaden the scope of teaching to include highly relevant management topics and skills. The materials are not only engaging for teachers, allowing them to introduce and develop new management communication skills in an ELT classroom; students are also motivated as they learn how to manage real professional communication challenges which they face at work on a daily basis.

Each title is designed primarily for work with both small and larger groups, but can also be used in one-to-one situations and has many features which will support self-study.

Across the eight units of each title, there is a strong focus on developing fluency and skills to communicate effectively in real work situations. There are opportunities to practise listening, reading and writing skills. The intercultural case studies in Section D are drawn from real-life examples and provide engaging discussion and problem-solving material for the ELT classroom.

There is online support for trainers (www.delta publishing.co.uk/resources) in the form of notes for each unit, which provide background information on the management topics and skills presented. There are also podcast interviews with the authors in which they discuss the ideas in the different titles, with practical tips for teachers on how to deal with the various topics and skills in the ELT classroom.

A final word

To both learner and teacher, we would like to express the hope that you find the materials stimulating, and that they help people to communicate more effectively at work.

Learning diary

Accelerate your learning by using this 'learning diary'. Make eight photocopies of this page, one for each unit. Note down important new words and expressions from the unit as you study. Make notes to help you remember any good advice you get on how to communicate and be effective across cultures. Then decide on some actions you can take to help to consolidate the things you have learned.

Unit number: _____

---

1 Language
Important (new) words and expressions for me from this unit are:

---

2 Professional communication skills
Important (new) expressions and communication tips for me from this unit are:

---

3 Intercultural competence
Important information/tips to be effective across cultures for me from this unit are:

---

4 Actions
To help me to consolidate all the learning points above, I need to:

Needs analysis

Introduction   You can use this Needs analysis to help you think about how to make the most of this course and to maximise your learning.

Managing your communication network   **1 Mapping your network**
First, think about who you communicate with in English. Draw a communication network which shows the important individuals or groups of people you communicate with. Follow the example and note down the medium of communication you use, e.g. face-to-face, phone, e-mail, teleconference, etc.

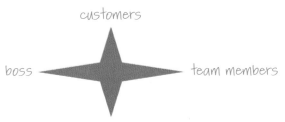

customers

boss ——————— *team members*

weekly team meetings, face to face, informal chats in corridor and during lunch, occasional evening social events. E-mail contact with team members in Brazil.

2 Improving your network
How effectively are you managing your network? Have you got your priorities right? Have you got the medium right in each case? Are you spending the right amount of time communicating with each individual or group?
Brainstorm some ideas below for ways in which you could handle your network more effectively.

I need to spend more time telephoning team members in Brazil, not just e-mailing them. This would build better relationships and get things done more quickly.

Your communication needs   What do you have to do in English, and how challenging is it? Build a communication profile by complete the following tables for project management skills, professional communication skills and interpersonal skills. Tick (✓) which task you have to do. Then note down how challenging you find it, use a scale of 1 to 5 (1 = very easy, 2 = easy, 3 = sometimes causes problems, 4 = challenging, 5 = very difficult). For any score of 3 or above, note down why the task is challenging.

Project management skills

skill	✓	scale of challenge
Defining a clear scope for the project		
Building relationships with team members		
Clarifying roles and responsibilities		
Getting information to complete tasks		
Communicating externally, e.g. engaging external stakeholders, and internally, e.g. with project sponsor, team members, etc.		
Completing tasks on time		
Other skills		

Professional communication skills

skill	✓	scale of challenge
Presenting		
Meeting		
Negotiating		
Telephoning		
Socialising		
E-mailing		

Interpersonal skills

skill	✓	scale of challenge
Building relationships		
Networking		
Building trust		
Influencing		
Making decisions		
Managing conflict		

Your language and communication challenges

Note down the three biggest language and communication challenges which you face:

1 ....
2 ....
3 ....

Your intercultural challenges

What are the biggest intercultural challenges which you face?

1 ....
2 ....
3 ....

Your current learning objectives

What would most help you to improve your ability to communicate effectively in an international context?

1 ....
2 ....
3 ....

Your future learning targets

As part of your learning plan, what targets can you fix for yourself? Start a learning diary (see page 5) and set targets for your future learning using this frame:

In one month's time, I aim to be able to ....

In three months' time, I aim to be able to ....

In six months' time, I aim to be able to ....

In one year's time, I aim to be able to ....

International project challenges

AIMS

A To understand success factors in international projects
B To improve presentation skills
C To reflect on the skills and qualities of project managers
D To develop flexible thinking for working across cultures

A Discussion and listening

Think about it   **1** Think of a major project in your own organisation or in other organisations. What were the objectives and main benefits of this project?

2 What do you think are the main challenges of managing a project?

Listen to this   **3** 🎧 ① Listen to an interview with Bärbel Pindl, an experienced project manager based in Hamburg in Germany, and Alessandro Pena, her team member based in Mexico City. They discuss their experiences of working on international projects together.

What do Bärbel and Alessandro specify as key skills and qualities for working on international projects?

4 🎧 ② Listen to the second part of the interview and answer these questions.
   a What does Bärbel say is the biggest challenge of working on international projects?
   b What did Bärbel find difficult about working in Mexico?
   c What does Alessandro say can be a mistake made by those coming from headquarters?
   d Bärbel says that sometimes the Mexican way is better. What is the 'Mexican way', and why is it better?

5 How important is it to stick to plans in project management? Why?

Focus on language   **6** Complete the text on page 9 on project management with words/phrases from this box.

> appoint   breakdown   dependencies   final testing
> lessons learned   project overview   project review report
> risk assessment   stakeholders   success factors

The five steps in the project management lifecycle

Every project management lifecycle contains five steps: Initiation, Planning, Execution, Monitoring/Control and Closure.

1 Initiation

In this first step, you provide a **(a)** .... in addition to the strategy, which you will implement to achieve the desired results. During the Initiation phase, you'll **(b)** .... a project manager, who in turn will select the project team members, based on their experience and skills.

2 Planning

This step should include a detailed **(c)** .... of project work to be done from the beginning to the end of the project, with the clear identification of any **(d)** .... between different stages of the project which could cause delays or difficulties. The Planning phase will also include a **(e)** .... , which will identify any foreseeable threats or dangers to the project. In short, the working process is defined, important people or **(f)** .... are identified, and reporting frequency and channels explained.

3 and 4 Execution and Monitoring/Control

During the Execution and Control phases, the planned solution is implemented. As the Execution and Control phases progress, groups across the organisation become more deeply involved in planning for the **(g)** .... , which will happen before going to production.

5 Closure

The Closure phase typically involves a formal **(h)** .... , which usually includes: a formal acceptance of the final product (by the client); a match between the client's initial requirements and the final delivered product; **(i)** .... , to summarise what has been discovered during the project; and the identification of **(j)** .... , which will be of benefit to future projects.

---

7 **Which verbs can you use to complete these short sentences describing different activities within a project? If you can, think of more than one verb for each sentence.**

We ...

a *set / agree / fix* .... a budget.

b .... a feasibility study.

c .... good results.

d .... the green light.

e .... a team.

f .... responsibilities.

g .... resources.

h .... a schedule.

i .... good progress.

j .... a few problems.

k .... the problems quickly.

l .... the project on time and on budget!

8 **How far do projects in your organisation follow a similar project lifecycle? Which of the phases is the most challenging? Why?**

Let's talk 9 **Take a few minutes to think about major projects with which you have been involved or are involved. Complete this chart, then share your project experiences with a partner. Collect as many good tips as you can from others about successful project management.**

MY PROJECT EXPERIENCE	
Types of project	
Your role in the projects	
Major successes/challenges in the projects (which stages went well or badly)	
From your experience, what you think are key success factors for projects	

Think about it 1 **Look at what different people say about their presentation style. How effective do you think these styles might be in different cultures? How would you describe your own style?**

> I'm very much an extrovert. I think audiences like my open and friendly style. I see myself as a bit of an entertainer.

> I like to have a very clear structure to my presentation. I think it helps audiences to understand.

> I hate audiences which constantly interrupt me. I tell them early on that questions are for the end.

> I like to be flexible and adjust to the expectations of the audience as much as I can.

Listen to this 2 🎧 ③ **Listen to Jack Svensson, the leader of a human resources project, beginning a presentation with his team after a meeting with the project sponsor. What presentation style does he decide to use? Why? How useful do you think it is to begin in this way?**

3 🎧 ④ **Listen to the next part of the presentation and complete this presentation slide.**

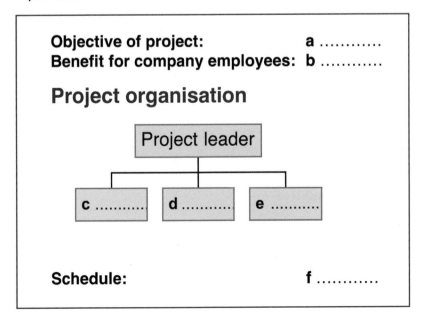

Objective of project: a ....
Benefit for company employees: b ....

Project organisation

Project leader

c ....   d ....   e ....

Schedule: f ....

4 🎧 **5** Listen to the third part of the presentation and answer these questions.

    a Which major challenges does Jack predict for the project?

    b Which actions does he recommend to deal with these challenges?

Focus on language **5 a** During the presentation, Jack demonstrated a number of useful techniques for presenting an overview of a project. Look at these examples, then match the expressions below with the correct headings (a–d).

    a Using structure

        I'd like to begin by ...

    b Highlighting key information

        Our objective is to ...

    c Describing project organisation

        We've divided the project into three parts.

    d Dealing with questions

        So, any questions on that so far?

    Does that answer the question?

    What I want to do now is to ...

    OK. If there are no more questions, I'll finish there.

    So, just to conclude, ...

    If you want me to clarify anything, just stop me.

    I'd like to say something important at the outset.

    We need to realise that ...

    I'd like to highlight/emphasise/stress that ...

    This part of the project is headed by ...

    As for project organisation, you can see ...

    The training team is responsible for ...

    So, you're asking if ... . Is that right?

    b Can you think of more phrases which you could use under these headings?

Let's talk **6** Use this framework to prepare a short project presentation (3–5 minutes) using some of the language from this section. You can describe a real project or invent one!

presenting a project	
Project name	
Main objectives and benefits of the project	
Project structure ● *organisation* ● *schedule*	
Main challenges and recommended actions to deal with these challenges	

When you are ready, go into small groups and give your presentation. Get feedback from your colleagues on how effective they thought it was.

Think about it 1 **What do you think are the three most important skills needed to be a good project manager? Why?**

Read this 2 **Read the article below on project management competence and answer these questions.**

  a Which three issues are said to be particularly challenging to manage?

  b What is 'intelligent disobedience'?

  c Why is killing a project listed as an example of intelligent disobedience?

  d What do you think 'fierce conversations' are, and why are they necessary?

  e At the end, it says 'Take a risk'. What is the risk?

Intelligent disobedience
The difference between good and great project managers

by Robert McGannon, PMP

The project manager (PM) is used to dealing with challenges. In some instances, however, these obstacles can be significant and include:
- uninvolved sponsors or key customers playing political games
- culture clashes that slow down project progress
- resistance to the changes in organisations which projects often create.

To manage such challenges, great PMs use 'intelligent disobedience'. This is what separates great PMs from average PMs.

So what is intelligent disobedience?
Can you imagine a guide dog that didn't have intelligent disobedience, walking into the street because its master told it to do so, despite the approaching car? Can you imagine a PM pushing forward with a project or a development that they knew would fail or is against wider organisational objectives? For PMs, intelligent disobedience is knowing when and how to depart from the norm in opinions, cultural standards and processes. Classical examples of a new disobedient PM practice might be:

- saying 'no' and proposing alternatives that challenge the status quo
- deciding you need to kill a 'pet' project as an alternative to failure
- sharing bad news and rewarding others who do the same
- breaking rules and guidelines which prevent project success
- taking over a problem project and demanding more authority within the company.

So how best to use intelligent disobedience?
Effective PMs need to have conversations with stakeholders that are often difficult – conversations that often cause us to lose sleep at night. Many avoid these conversations or 'sugar-coat' them in an effort to preserve the current relationship with stakeholders. According to Susan Scott (2002), the author of *Fierce conversations*, if we are having 'careful' conversations with our stakeholders, then the nature of our relationship with those stakeholders will never be fully truthful and our chance of success decreases. Take a risk and try intelligent disobedience. The results can be well worth it!

3 **Discuss these questions in pairs.**

  a How easy do you think it is to be disobedient?

  b In your own organisation, how far is it possible to disagree with managers and break rules or guidelines?

  c Do you think honesty and openness is always the best policy, or is it sometimes better to 'sugar-coat' conversations with stakeholders to maintain relationships? Why?

Focus on language **4** Complete the description below of a project manager's role with the correct form of the verbs in the box.

break down	design	draw up	ensure	manage
meet	recruit	run	track	write

Your role as Project Manager entails responsibility for **(a)** .... all kinds of projects. As the manager, you would have to **(b)** .... the smooth running of the project. This would include **(c)** .... the right team of workers and specialists.

Once you have **(d)** .... a project to meet client requirements, selected your team and **(e)** .... the plans, various management tasks are expected. These include **(f)** .... reports and making sure that each project element **(g)** .... according to plan, making changes where needed, dealing with tenders, budgetary estimates and speaking with clients or users of the project.

Part of your work involves using particular project management methods required by the company. Whatever the method, you will need to **(h)** .... the project into stages and **(i)** .... its progress as **(j)** .... tight deadlines is important. You would also use specialised computer software to help with scheduling, costing and risk analysis.

5 How important do you think it is for people in a project team to discuss and understand the different jobs and roles that everyone has? Why? Compare your answer to the project tip on page 88.

6 Look at the sentences below describing skills and interests for good project managers. Match each of the words in bold to a word in the box.

commitment	deployment	focus	manage	monitoring
motivated	orally	people	skills	structured

To be a good project manager, you must:

a be highly organised with a logical, **methodical** approach to work.
b have problem-solving **capabilities** to respond to a range of challenges.
c be a self-starter and **driven** to reach targets.
d have the stamina and **determination** to cope with a busy schedule.
e have planning skills to **co-ordinate** several simultaneous projects.
f have an understanding of budgetary control, scheduling and resource **allocation** and management.
g have strong **interpersonal** leadership and negotiation skills.
h be able to communicate well with people at all levels, both **verbally** and in writing.
i have technical skills relevant to the **scope** of the project.
j understand techniques for **controlling** programmes.

7 Look back to your ideas at the beginning of this unit and write sentences to describe the qualities you thought were important for project management.

Let's talk **8** Imagine that you are meeting a new colleague in an international project. You want to describe your current role to them so that they understand what you do, the skills you have and the pressures of your job. This will help them to work with you during the project. Plan what you will say using the chart below, then go into groups and describe your jobs, making sure you ask the other members of the group plenty of follow-up questions, so you understand their working lives.

my current role profile	
main responsibilities:	
reporting lines:	
main challenges:	
key skills to do the job:	
likes and dislikes:	

D Intercultural competence: Testing your intercultural competence

1 Take a close look at this photo and write some sentences which describe what you see (in fewer than 75 words). Spend three minutes completing the exercise. Then compare your answers with a partner.

2 🎧 **6** You are going to hear an interview with George Williams, an American expert on intercultural competence, in which he discusses the task you did in Exercise 1 and why he thinks it is important as a learning activity. Listen and answer these questions.

    a What mistake do people usually make when describing the picture?

    b Why is this dangerous when working across cultures?

    c What tip does George give for working across cultures?

    d How can this benefit those working in projects?

3 **How far do you agree with George Williams? Why?**

4 a **George Williams describes how groups can use creative thinking to support problem-solving in meetings. Look at these five strategies for promoting creative thinking during a discussion. Match each expression below (a–g) to one of the strategies (1–5).**

    Strategies to promote creative thinking during a discussion

    1 Asking for creative ideas from others

    2 Investigating the ideas of others

    3 Commenting on interpretations

    4 Introducing alternative interpretations

    5 Recommending actions based on specific interpretations

    a Does this mean that ...?

    b I can see what you're saying because ...

    c As we can't be sure of that, the first thing we need to do is ...

    d Interesting, why do you say that?

    e Any thoughts on this?

    f What do you think is happening here?

    g Could we look at it another way and say that ...?

    b **How many more phrases can you add to express the same ideas?**

5 **Work in groups and discuss the two cases on page 15 involving misunderstanding across cultures. Try to use open and flexible thinking and encourage others to do the same, in order to discover possible explanations for the problems and their solutions. Use these questions to structure your discussion, then compare your conclusions to the case summaries on page 88.**

    a What is the main problem?

    b How far is culture a factor in how people are thinking and behaving?

    c If you were the project sponsor, what would you do to solve each problem?

Case 1

A Baltic project group starts to get irritated with its Swedish manager (recently appointed after a takeover of the Baltic company by a Swedish group). The manager is passive and fails to give clear instructions on how to do technical tasks during a key phase of their project. The group decides to tell the Swedish leader at the next team meeting that it needs more effective leadership.

Case 2

Three Australian research-and-development project team members are losing patience in meetings with their French colleague from marketing. During discussions held every Monday, the colleague keeps dominating the meeting and never sticks to the point. He uses complex and irrelevant arguments about products which are impossible to develop within company deadlines. The team decides to introduce communication rules for discussion at the next meeting, to stop this kind of time-wasting during critical meetings.

Case study: A question of missing data

Background   Jack is a senior financial controller, working for a global manufacturer within its finance head office in New York. As part of a recent international project to improve managing the global finance functions, he has been asked to collect local financial data from country heads around the world and compile a new global report. He has travelled to several countries to meet local Heads of Finance and explain the new process. But budget is limited, and so fewer trips have been made in the last six months. He has not yet been to India, although several video and telephone conference calls have been held to explain the situation.

Situation   Jack has asked Paresh, the local Head of Finance in India, to supply the Indian country data to the project several times. He has relied mainly on e-mails (see below) to make the request, using what he sees as a polite and professional tone. Jack has also spoken to Paresh by phone about this problem. Despite repeated promises made by Paresh over recent weeks, nothing has happened. Jack is getting increasingly late delivering his own work and is becoming very frustrated. He decides to raise the matter with his director in New York, to speed up the process.

E-mail 1

> Paresh – I really need that data asap, as discussed last week. Can you confirm you can let me have it?

E-mail 2

> Hi Jack
> Busy here, but understood. I will get the data to you as soon as I can.
> Best regards
> Paresh

Task   In groups, discuss these questions.

a What do you think could be the main problem(s)?

b What do you think of Jack's approach to solve the problem?

c What would you do in this position?

d Which intercultural skills do you think are important to solve such a case?

One person in each group should take notes on the discussion and give a short summary of the group's views.

E Language reference

Read through the key words and phrases below from this unit. Add any other useful words and expressions which you feel are important for you to learn. Make sure you find the time to review the words and phrases regularly and to use them at work.

Project roles/responsibilities
steering committee
project leader/manager*
team member
stakeholder

sponsor
sub-project leader/manager
project management office (PMO)
user (customer)

*used interchangeably in this book

Project leader skills
highly organised
methodical approach to work
self-motivated

logical
problem-solving capabilities
driven to reach targets

He has stamina and determination.
She can co-ordinate complex projects.
He has good interpersonal skills.

Project lifecycle
initiation
planning
execution

monitoring/control
closure

Verbs for project activities
set a budget
achieve good results
form a team
allocate resources
make good progress
solve problems quickly
run according to plan
start up a project
take on people

run a feasibility study
get the green light
define responsibilities
fix a schedule
run into a few problems.
complete the project on time and on budget
write up a report
draw up plans
meet client requirements

Miscellaneous
a sub-project
a milestone
a deadline
lessons learned
a risk assessment
a budgetary estimate

a requirement
a project schedule
a dependency
a success factor
a project report
a tender

Writing task **Choose one of these situations. Try to include at least ten of the project words above in your e-mail.**

1 Your manager has informed you of an opportunity to work on an international project at head office based on your current responsibilities. The project manager is interested to learn more about you and has requested that you send a short e-mail describing your experience of working on international projects as soon as possible. Write the e-mail, asking any questions which you feel necessary at this stage.

2 Your international project manager is due back from a week's holiday tomorrow. Send a short e-mail, informing them of your main activities over the last seven days and any problems which arose.

F Project management tips and personal action plan

1 Take a few minutes to reflect on these project management tips. How far do you agree with each one? Which do you think is most important, and which ideas are most useful?

TIP 1

Prioritise relationship-building in the early phases of the project. When working internationally, there are fewer opportunities to get to know project members and build necessary levels of understanding and trust.
Idea to help relationship-building:
● Build extensive get-to-know activities into the project kick-off meeting as a way to allow people to understand more deeply the personalities and cultural background of team members.

TIP 2

See diversity in project teams as an opportunity rather than a problem. International teams often face the challenge of greater diversity in terms of expectations of teamwork, leadership, decision-making, etc. But multiple perspectives can offer greater chance of innovation.
Idea to help teams make the most of their diversity:
● State at the beginning of each meeting that different points of view are valued and welcome. This can help to maintain a positive atmosphere, even when people disagree.

TIP 3

Avoid getting drawn into project politics. International projects can be highly political, with senior managers fighting behind the scenes, some supporting and some undermining the project. In this situation, it is important to show courage and give an honest point of view.
Idea to help manage the politics of projects:
● It can be useful to have a mentor in the organisation to give advice on key decisions and during difficult moments.

---

2 What other ideas for working on projects have you got from studying this unit?

Personal action plan 3 Think about what you have learned from this unit. Note down two or three important points which you want to apply to your own job (*What?*). Then create a schedule to implement your learning (*When?*) and think about the best way to check that you have successfully applied the ideas (*How?*).

4 Discuss your personal action plan and adapt it if necessary, based on any useful feedback you get.

	what I learned and want to apply in my job	when/how I will apply this in my job	how I will check if I have applied it
1			
2			
3			

2 Getting it right from the start

AIMS

A To understand different approaches to planning
B To develop relationship-building skills
C To develop skills for working virtually
D To consider the concept of time across cultures

A Discussion and listening

Think about it

1 Why is planning important for projects? What kinds of things need to be planned to ensure a successful start for a project?

2 The kick-off meeting is one of the first big events to be planned in a project. Discuss these questions.

    a In your experience, what are the main objectives of a project kick-off meeting?

    b If you were planning a one-day meeting, what kind of things would you include in the agenda?

Listen to this

3 🎧 **7** **Listen to an interview with Meera Patel, a senior project leader who has worked on many construction projects in India over the last five years.**

    a What does Meera say about the importance of project planning in India?

    b What kind of planning does Meera recommend for international projects? Why?

    c What happens if you plan too much?

4 a 🎧 **8** **Listen to the second part of the interview, in which Meera discusses a kick-off meeting which she is planning for next month.**

    a What is the most important objective of this meeting?

    b What does Meera describe as a 'second objective' of the meeting?

    c What things will Meera say to introduce herself at the meeting?

    d Who was invited to her last kick-off meeting, and why? What happened?

    e What does Meera always organise for the first evening of a kick-off meeting? Why?

b Which of Meera's ideas do you agree/disagree with? Why?

Focus on language   **5** Complete the e-mail below with the correct form of the planning verbs from the box.

allocate	appoint	approve	assemble	co-operate
co-ordinate	order	proceed	sort out	submit

Dear Matt
Good news! You know that I **(a)** .... the project proposal last week. Well, I got the news this morning that the board has **(b)** .... it, so we can **(c)** ....
I have been formally **(d)** .... as project leader, but I now need to **(e)** .... a team which can get the job done. I would really appreciate it if you could help me **(f)** .... things over the next few weeks, particularly on the staffing and logistics side. Regarding logistics, we've been **(g)** .... an office, but I need to **(h)** .... quite a lot of equipment so we can actually get started. Could you get in touch with Peter in Purchasing and work closely with him to **(i)** .... what we need? The two of you usually **(j)** .... so well.
I'll give you a call a little later today to talk things through.

6 Can you think of any other words with a similar meaning to the words in the box that you could use to complete the e-mail?

7 a Meera discussed the importance of planning a strong personal introduction at kick-off meetings. Look at these notes made by a project member planning her personal introduction at a forthcoming kick-off meeting. Circle the correct word to complete them.

Professional
I'm a brand manager in Germany. I have a strong **(a)** *career / background* in marketing. My main **(b)** *expert / expertise* is brand management, which might be useful in the project when it comes to communicating with senior management.

Role in project
In terms of my role in the project, my main **(c)** *responsibility / work* is to make sure at the end of the day that we can sell the product successfully. And so the main **(d)** *outcome / delivery* of my part of the project will be an advertising concept and campaign which will convince customers to buy our product.

Personal information
On a personal **(e)** *note / touch*, I'm **(f)** *originally / originated* from Regensburg. And when **(g)** *I'm not working / I don't work*, you'll probably find me in the ocean somewhere, as my big passion is scuba diving.

Working style
Regarding working style, I can say that I'm very well organised. I like structure and planning. I always try very **(h)** *hard / hardly* to meet my deadlines and I expect the same from others, too. I can be a bit reserved, quiet maybe, but I'm very interested in people. I like to support people, but it can take me a bit of time to open up. So please **(i)** *be / have* patience with me.

Positive comment
And a final comment, I'd like to say that I'm very happy to be **(j)** *involved / engaged* in the project, because I think the work will be interesting and is very important for the future of the organisation.

b 🎧 **9** Listen to check your answers.

c What do you think of the above as a model for a personal introduction in a kick-off meeting? What do you (not) like? Why? What other things could you say?

Let's talk   **8** You have to plan and then give a short personal introduction at the start of the kick-off meeting of a new international project.
- Take a few minutes to prepare what you would like to say.
- Form groups and give your personal introductions.
- Take notes as the other people give their personal introductions and give feedback about what you like in terms of:
  – what they said (content)
  – how they said it (style of communication).

Think about it 1 **When you are participating in an international project, who do you need to build relationships with? Complete this diagram.**

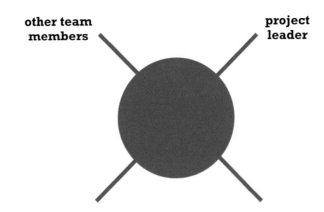

2 **We can build relationships with people in many different ways. Look at these comments and discuss which methods you use with people at work, and why. How do you think relationship-building might differ across cultures?**

> We have lunch regularly together at work.

> We sometimes meet up after work to do sport.

> I regularly offer support and advice to my colleagues.

> Sometimes little gifts are a nice way to build relationships.

> I ask the team members and their families over for dinner at the weekend.

> I try to ask more personal questions to get to know the private side of the person.

> For me, it's about giving personal facts about yourself to build a more intimate relationship.

Listen to this 3 🎧 **10** Julia Jäger is meeting Vadim Abramov, a colleague in a project to develop new cosmetic products for the European market. Listen to their conversation and answer these questions.

 a Which general topic does Julia ask Vadim about first?

 b What does she then ask about the project?

 c What problem do they discuss?

 d What does Julia recommend that Vadim does?

4 🎧 **11** **Now listen to a telephone call between Julia and Vadim.**

 a Why does Julia call Vadim?

 b What suggestion does she make to support him?

 c What do they agree to do at the end of the call?

5 **What do you like about Julia's style of conversation with Vadim? In what ways is her style different to your own style?**

Focus on language 6 **Complete this conversation by adding appropriate words in line with the marginal notes. Note that in most cases, more than one answer is possible.**

Jan: Hey, long time no see! What are you **(a)** .... these days? *(Open with a general question)*

Bob: Well, I'm fine. Keeping busy. How **(b)** .... ? *(Return the question)*

Jan: I'm fine. I've been preparing the supplier data for the meeting today. It's a big job, I can tell you.

Bob: I can **(c)** .... *(Show understanding)*

Jan: Yes, I managed to get it all done last night, so I'm ready for today.

Bob: Was it **(d)** .... to get all the data? *(Ask about the project)*

Jan: Absolutely. Quite a few departments didn't want to give us the information, but we got there eventually.

Bob: What was the **(e)** .... exactly? *(Ask a follow-up question)*

Jan: Well, people didn't want to tell us how much they were paying, in case they got criticised for paying too much. In fact, the data shows we're actually getting most of our training for a very good price.

Bob: **(f)** .... ! *(Make a positive comment)*

Jan: How is the **(g)** .... of the project going? *(Ask about the project)*

Bob: It's fine, but we're struggling a little bit with IT. They're not really co-operating.

(Offer advice) Jan: **(h)** .... raising the issue with senior management? Would that help?

Bob: I think it would make things worse, to be honest.

Jan: I know that IT can be difficult. I had the **(i)** .... issue with them last year. *(State similar experience)*

(Offer support) **(j)** .... anything I can do from my side?

Bob: Can we talk about it over dinner tonight? There are one or two things you might be able to help with.

Jan: Sure, no problem. Let's talk about it later.

7 **Offering advice to team members is a good way to demonstrate commitment to them and to the project. Towards the end of the conversation, Jan offers some advice to Bob:**

What about raising the issue with senior management?

With a partner, describe some challenges you are facing at work and offer advice to deal with them.

Let's talk 8 **With a partner, use the ideas in this section to create short conversations and improve your relationship-building skills.**

Student A: Turn to page 89.
Student B: Turn to page 97.

- Ask a mix of social and professional questions.
- Comment on and ask follow-up questions to the answers, to maintain a positive conversation.
- Offer help with any problems that are mentioned if possible.

When you finish talking, take a minute to write down a few comments on what you liked about the conversation. Then discuss your comments.

Think about it   **1** A 'virtual' project team is a group of people who work across distance and organisational boundaries, using technology such as e-mail and video conferencing as their main method of communication. Why do you think companies are establishing more and more virtual teams?

   2 What do you think makes working in a virtual project team attractive and challenging for leaders and team members?

Read this   **3** Read the article below on managing virtual teams and match these headings to the correct paragraphs.

     a Keep team members visible   **d** Include face-to-face time

     b Plan for virtual success   **e** Recognise people

     c Establish group norms   **f** Keep the project/activity visible

Managing virtual teams

Research provides clear recommendations on how to manage virtual teams.

1 ....

Schedule an initial face-to-face meeting for the team members to get to know each other and socialise. Given that team performance is based on trust, it is important to create time for people to get to know each other professionally and socially.

2 ....

Keep team members informed where a project/activity is along the project timeline, and what people are expected to contribute and when. A project website, with all the relevant project data, can be a good way to provide team members with a single access point to all they need to know about a project.

3 ....

Set ground rules about how team members communicate and interact. The combination of multiple time zones, busy team members and electronic communications will create communication delays. Creating protocols for e-mail is particularly important. For example, the team may decide to agree to acknowledge any e-mail communication within 24 hours. We all know that it is very easy to create misunderstanding and irritation if there is no response to e-mails.

4 ....

Use the Internet or appropriate software to store and share team members' calendars. While this could be difficult to keep up to date on a daily basis, it should be possible to include all regular meetings and absences such as holidays and business travel.

5 ....

Recognise performance – anything from a simple 'thank you' through to a more formal reward such as a bonus. Recognition builds commitment by making people's actions visible to their peers and therefore making it difficult to deny or ignore. In a virtual context, public recognition can be given during video conferences or via e-mail, with other team members copied in.

6 ....

When managing virtual teams, you don't have the luxury of benefiting from spontaneous, in-the-corridor meetings that happen when you all work in one location. Out of sight frequently leads to out of mind. However, leaders have to make these connections happen in other ways. They should arrange regular visits or frequent telephone calls and e-mails, so that they can track progress and keep people motivated. Team leaders sometimes complain that limited time and budgets make it difficult to maintain such connections, but with planning, discipline and a little creativity ... anything is possible!

4 Read the article again and answer these questions.

     a How can virtual team members build trust with each other, according to the article?

     b How can a project website support a virtual project team?

     c The article suggests that 'creating protocols for e-mail communication is particularly important'. Why do you think it says 'particularly important'?

     d How should team leaders give positive feedback to team members in a virtual environment, according to the article?

     e In the final paragraph, it says that 'Out of sight frequently leads to out of mind'. What challenge for international leaders is described by this, and what solution is suggested?

5 The final paragraph says that it is the responsibility of the project leader to manage the virtual team challenge. How far do you agree with this? How far do think the project team members can also help to make the team work effectively? What should they do?

Focus on language 6 Effective e-mail communication is essential for virtual teams. How would you assess the effectiveness of these e-mails? Compare your ideas with the commentary on page 89.

E-mail 1

Hi Michael
I've been reading the first reports we all received from users following the pilot phase of the new office design project here in Romania. It's very disappointing, with quite a lot of negative feedback.
I think this feedback could delay the go-live of the main project.
Ruxandra

E-mail 2

Pete
You still haven't sent me the project schedule overview I asked for last week. You must send it this afternoon, because I need it to prepare my presentation to the board here.
Dan

7 How would you change the e-mails in Exercise 6 to make them clearer and/or more polite? Compare your answers with others in the class.

8 Many e-mails for internal communication are very informal. However, a more formal style may sometimes be useful. Complete the second sentence in each of these pairs of sentences so that each expresses the same idea as the first sentence, but in a more formal style.

a Thanks for getting in touch last week.
With __reference__ to your e-mail __dated__ 4 February, 2012, ...

b I just wanted to say cheers for your help last week.
I am _____ to _____ thanks for your _____ at the meeting last Friday.

c I can make the meeting.
I am _____ to confirm that I am able to _____ the meeting.

d Sorry, but Jane can't come.
I _____ to say that Jane is _____ to attend.

e I can ask Peter to come instead.
If you _____ , I would be _____ to ask Peter to attend in her place.

f Could you send details of the hotel?
I would _____ it if you could _____ me have details of the accommodation.

g Sorry, I forgot to tell you about Jane before.
I must _____ for not informing you about Jane _____ .

h Come back to me if you need more on this.
Do not _____ to contact me if you need _____ information.

i See you next week.
I very much look _____ to _____ you next week.

9 Which of the above phrases do you use in your e-mails? Which other typical phrases do you use?

Let's write 10 Choose two or three tasks from this list and write an e-mail for each. Add information from your own work context (e.g. name of receiver, facts and figures, etc.) where necessary.

a Arranging or rearranging a meeting
b Requesting information
c Requesting help with a problem
d Providing help to solve a problem

When you have finished, work in groups to evaluate the different e-mails.

D Intercultural competence: Attitudes to time

1 Edward T. Hall, an American anthropologist, found that cultures can differ significantly in attitudes to time. Read this example of a culture clash concerning time. Do you think the American manager is right to feel irritated? Why? / Why not?

At a multinational company with headquarters in Switzerland, an important meeting of department managers is scheduled for 2 p.m. One of these managers, an American, is approaching the meeting room and is stopped by one of his staff. 'Excuse me, boss,' she says, 'but I'm having some trouble with this report. Could you help me?' 'Well, I'm on my way to a meeting right now. I'll stop by your office at 4.30 and we'll talk about it then.'

At the other end of the building, a Brazilian manager is also headed to the same meeting. One of his staff stops him, too, with the same request for help. 'Sure, what's the problem?' asks the Brazilian manager, and the two of them stand in the corridor discussing the problem for ten minutes until it is solved. The Brazilian arrives at the meeting over five minutes late, but isn't worried at all by this. The American, however, is irritated by his colleague's lateness.

2 🎧 **12** Listen to Mikhail Greshnev, a construction engineer from Moscow, describing problems which arose in a big project to modernise an aluminium plant.

   a What problem with time does he describe?

   b How does he explain the cause of the problem?

   c How does he try to solve the problem?

3 🎧 **13** Now listen to Jesús Ortiz, the project leader of a group of external South American consultants working on the Russian project. How does his point of view differ to Mikhail's?

4 Jesús say that it is important to be flexible when working with people who have very different attitudes to time. How far do you agree with this? Why?

5 a Take a moment to profile your own attitudes to time in the workplace. Look at these statements and decide how far you agree.

   I like to plan my week ahead in detail.

   I prefer to concentrate on doing one task at a time.

   I always like to have a clear agenda for meetings.

   I sometimes arrive late for meetings.

   I am happy to miss a deadline for the sake of higher quality.

   I am tolerant if others miss deadlines or are late for meetings.

   I think you can waste a lot of time planning too far ahead.

   I am happy to reschedule meetings at the last minute.

   b Now discuss and compare your responses with others in a group. Ask the group to suggest ways in which you individually might show more flexibility and tolerance to others' different attitudes to time at work. Write down any ideas you agree with.

Case study: A question of time

Background Birgit Pleuger works for one of the world's leading financial services companies. She is based in Switzerland and is leading an international project called 'Go Car', to develop internet-based products for car insurance.

The project is scheduled to last for nine months. It had its kick-off six weeks ago, and it went very well. However, differences have begun to develop in the team, and Birgit is getting worried.

Situation Birgit recently received e-mails from two members of her team. Petra Blattner, based in Switzerland, was complaining about Franco Peroni, who is based in the Milan office.

To: Birgit Pleuger
From: Petra Blattner
Subject: Franco Peroni

Dear Birgit

Regarding my side of the project, things are pretty much up to date. However, Franco has missed a lot of deadlines recently, which has delayed the piloting of the website design in the Italian region. I've tried to clarify my expectations as the person responsible for design, but he is not very open when I try to discuss this with him. He just doesn't seem to recognise the need to meet deadlines.

To be honest, I'm getting a bit fed up with his lack of professionalism, but will try to deal with it constructively when I talk to him tomorrow. I'll keep you informed.
Petra

To: Birgit Pleuger
From: Franco Peroni
Subject: Re: Go Car issues

Dear Birgit

Great to hear from you. The family is fine and I hope yours is, too. On the project front, we're moving forward. I'm a bit concerned that we may be moving too fast and some of the deadlines are totally unrealistic. I think there are still problems with the website design, and I'm not really happy to pilot it with users here until things are sorted out.

Petra is not very open to this point of view, and I can see us having a real disagreement eventually. Do you think you could speak to her? She's creating a lot of pressure, which is demotivating for my team here.
Grazie!
Franco

Task **Discuss these questions.**

a What do you think could be the main issues here?

b How would you answer these e-mails?

c Would you talk to these people individually or together or both? Why?

d Which intercultural skills are important to solve such a case?

Read through the key words and phrases below from this unit. Add any other useful words and expressions which you feel are important for you to learn. Make sure you find the time to review the words and phrases regularly and to use them at work.

Project meetings

fix

organise/reorganise

come to / attend a meeting

cancel (participation at a meeting)

schedule/reschedule

arrange/re-arrange

confirm attendance at a meeting

dial into a meeting

Planning verbs

allocate	co-ordinate	schedule
appoint	define	set up
approve	order	sort out
assemble	organise	structure
co-operate	proceed	submit

Verbs with *problems*

solve	find a solution to
deal with	find a workaround for
tackle	avoid
escalate	minimise

Working in a virtual team

It's important to:

- spend time getting to know each other
- socialise
- set / agree to work to ground rules
- clarify expectations
- keep people informed
- create clear communication protocols
- acknowledge e-mails
- show/build trust
- recognise performance
- keep people up to date.

Writing task   **Choose one of these situations. Try to include at least ten of the project words above in your e-mail.**

1   Your project sponsor has asked you to e-mail some ideas to organise a forthcoming international kick-off meeting. The project will bring together the heads of HR from the global organisation in Milan to begin a project called 'Business partnering'. The project aims to redesign global HR into a more internal customer-friendly service organisation. Over ten nationalities will be present at the one-day event in Milan.

2   Your colleague in London promised last week to e-mail you a report showing UK business-unit profit and loss over the last three years. The e-mail has still not arrived, but you need the report to create a presentation for the project sponsor. E-mail again to request the data.

F Project management tips and personal action plan

1 Take a few minutes to reflect on these project management tips. How far do you agree
with each one? Which do you think is most important, and which ideas are most useful?

TIP 1

Balance strong organisation with flexible planning, particularly in the early
project phases, until you are sure of the environment. International projects tend to be
characterised by more uncertainty and complexity than domestic projects. This can
make it difficult to schedule and organise your project work effectively.
Idea to help flexible planning:
● Plan short-term milestones rather than long-term ones. Meet regularly to review
   progress towards these milestones and to set further realistic short-term deadlines.

TIP 2

Use the kick-off meeting as an opportunity build self-awareness and mutual
appreciation among the team. Encourage team members to talk to each other to learn
about each other's professional skills and personal interests outside work, and thus
start to build trust. Perhaps even post profiles of team members in a shared web space
for everyone to view.
Idea to help build the team:
● Use an external trainer to provide intercultural awareness or intercultural
   communication training. It can be a great way to kick-start international team
   co-operation.
Idea to help teams make the most of their diversity:
● State at the beginning of each meeting that different points of view are valued and
   welcome. This can help to maintain a positive atmosphere, even when people
   disagree.

TIP 3

Define ground rules for the team, particularly around communication and attitudes to
time. Clarify expectations, for example, of e-mail communication – what is the right
style, how quickly should people respond, etc.
Idea to help create clear team guidelines:
● Point out to native speakers of English that they need to write and speak a simple
   international English which is easy for non-native-speaker colleagues to
   understand.

Personal action plan 2 Think about what you have learned from this unit. Note down two or three important
points which you want to apply to your own job (*What?*). Then create a schedule to
implement your learning (*When?*) and think about the best way to check that you have
successfully applied the ideas (*How?*).

3 Discuss your personal action plan and adapt it if necessary, based on any useful feedback
you get.

	what I learned and want to apply in my projects	when/how I will apply this in my projects	how I will check if I have applied it
1			
2			
3			

3 Managing people in projects

AIMS

A To understand the challenges of managing people
B To improve influencing skills
C To develop strategies for managing senior stakeholders
D To work with different leadership styles across cultures

A Discussion and listening

Think about it **1** Look at this quote about managing projects from Jan Ivarsson, a project manager from Norway. How far do you agree with him?

> The main challenge for me has always been managing the people side of projects and not the technical side. People are always more complex than machines, believe me.

2 What do you think could be the main people-management challenge in international projects? Why? Compare your answers in groups.

Listen to this **3** 🎧 **14** Listen to a group of project managers talking about the team-management challenges they face. Complete this table to summarise what they say are the main challenges and what they see as ways to manage these challenges.

internal team challenges	solutions
1	1
2	2

4 🎧 **15** Now listen to the second part of the discussion, in which the team reflects on managing people outside the project team, and answer these questions.

a Who does Vladimir identify as the 'key person' for him in most of his projects?

b What example from a recent project does Vladimir give to show the importance of this person?

c Who does Kate identify as important? What negative influence on the project does she say that this group can have?

d What does Kate do to manage this group of people?

5 Do you agree that it is important to manage the people identified in the discussion? What other ideas do you have for managing these particular challenges? What other challenges not mentioned do you think are important?

Focus on language **6 a During the interview, motivation was mentioned as an important people-management issue. Complete each of the comments on motivation below with the correct word from the box.**

acknowledging	advance	benefit	conditions	driver
empowerment	incentivise	model	praise	rewards

    a We managed motivation very well in my last project by having a series of .... available for team members who reached their targets.

    b I think it's important to .... people to work hard with things like bonuses, training and even team-building activities.

    c Personally, I don't believe you increase motivation by paying people. I think that recognition, ... when people do a good job, is much more important.

    d Intrinsic motivation is the most important .... for individuals. As a leader, you need to know what pushes people to do things, and then give people a role which connects to these needs.

    e I'm a great believer in delegation or .... Trusting people with responsibility is the best motivator, from my experience.

    f In my culture, it's very important to .... frequently. If you're not giving good feedback, you're basically telling people that they are doing a bad job.

    g People need inspiration. Project leaders need to .... the behaviour that they expect from others, otherwise they can't demand it.

    h You can get people to work hard in projects if they feel it will .... their careers in some way.

    i Don't forget basic things such as working .... when talking about motivation. Many of my project team spend so much time travelling that asking them to go economy class would really demotivate them.

    j Make sure you can answer some basic questions people will ask themselves when you want them to join your project. *What's in it for me? What's the* .... *for me to work in this project?*

b Which of the above ideas do you agree and disagree with? Why?

7 You are going to listen to a short discussion between two people about motivation. Before you listen, match up the two parts of each question.

    a How motivated do you   **1** in the group or one to one?
    b And how happy   **2** about my style that demotivates you?
    c Am I asking   **3** feedback should I be giving?
    d Is there anything   **4** and the team feel at the moment?
    e What kind of   **5** people to do too much?
    f Is feedback best given   **6** are you with my style of leadership?

8 🎧 16 Now listen to the discussion between Sabrina van Aubel, who is leading an international automotive project in Mexico, and one of her team members, José Romeu. Sabrina is asking José about his motivation, because she is worried that stress levels are too high. Note down José's answers to her questions (see Exercise 7).

Let's talk **9 In pairs, role-play a discussion between a business coach and an employee (coachee). The coach should help the coachee to define some ideas to deal with the problems identified. When you have finished, change roles.**

    Student A: Turn to page 88.
    Student B: Turn to page 95.

B Communication skills: Influencing

Think about it 1 Test your influencing skills. Read the activity below and, in small groups, see how good you are at influencing your partner.

Give me the diamond!

 Form small groups of three or four. One person pretends to hold a very expensive diamond in their hand. Another person in the group has three minutes to influence this person to give them the diamond.

 The other observer(s) should follow the conversation and take a note of which influencing tactics are used, and which seem to be most successful.

 After the conversation, stop and discuss. Then change roles and repeat the exercise.

● When you have finished, decide which influencing tactics were most effective, and why.

2 Who do you have to influence at work? Describe a situation when you were successful in persuading someone to do something, or were persuaded yourself. Which strategies were effective in achieving this?

Listen to this 3 🎧 **17** Madelyn Alvares works for Chemtro, a leading chemical manufacturer based in Boston, USA. As Head of Health and Safety, she is leading a project to create a new e-learning training programme for all employees on plant safety. Listen to a telephone call between Madelyn and Haruki Takahashi, a project manager responsible for the design part of the e-learning programme.

    a What is the reason for Haruki's call?

    b Which arguments does Haruki use to influence Madelyn?

    c How successful do you think he is? Why?

4 Madelyn wants to influence her project sponsor, Sam Jackson, to delay the project. What arguments could she use to persuade him? What do you think will be the main objections from the sponsor? How could Madelyn deal with these objections?

5 🎧 **18** Listen to the call between Madelyn and Sam, and compare your ideas with what actually happens. How successful do you think she is?

6 Match each of these influencing strategies (a–f) with one of the explanations (1–6) below.

    a Ask questions
    b Explain benefits
    c Look at the environment
    d Be convinced yourself
    e Offer support
    f Warn of consequences

    1 If we're sure about something, it persuades others.
    2 What others do and why – maybe we should follow.
    3 If others feel you understand them, they are more easily persuaded.
    4 We can influence by pointing out unseen risks.
    5 People are often convinced to do something if you support them.
    6 Show what positives are behind your argument.

7 🎧 **19–24** **Listen to six short dialogues. Which influencing strategy from Exercise 6 (a–f) is represented in each one?**

8 Work with a partner and see if you can influence them to:
- give a presentation instead of you at a conference next month
- work next weekend to speed up part of a project.

When you finish, give feedback to the person who was influencing on what they did well. Then change roles.

9 You are going to role-play a meeting between a project leader and a team member, regarding a request for time off.

Project leader: See below.
Team member: Turn to page 98 .

Read your role cards and prepare for the meeting using some of the influencing strategies from this section.
Hold the meeting, then give feedback to each other on how effectively influencing strategies were used.

Project leader

One of your team wants to take a six-week break from your project in order to complete a personal goal (to do some voluntary work in South America).
This request has come at a very bad time. The project is behind schedule, and everyone is working very hard (too hard). You think that agreeing to this request would give out the wrong messages to other team members.
You want to find a solution which satisfies the team member in some way and is good for the project. Ideally, the staff member will postpone this dream for a couple of years.

C Professional skills: Stakeholder analysis

Think about it 1 Discuss these questions.

a Who are or were the key stakeholders in projects you have been involved in?

b Who are or were the most important, and why?

Read this 2 Stakeholder analysis identifies the people or groups that are likely to affect or be affected by a proposed action. It describes their likely impact on the action and the impact the action will have on them.

The stakeholder analysis below was prepared by the leader of a project which aims to outsource financial controlling activities, such as the regular collection of financial data for monthly reporting. The project is designed to reduce costs (around 30 jobs will go) and allow the finance department to focus on more complex priority tasks.

Complete the analysis with these stakeholder actions.

1 Contact Learning and Development to get support to create training programmes.

2 Provide training in conflict management.

3 Get a mentor who can help to develop understanding of the project.

4 Plan regular monthly meetings for the rest of the year.

5 Offer outplacement support early for those who have to leave the company.

6 Set up a workshop to provide training in existing internal processes.

stakeholder	stake in the project	stakeholder attitudes and related project risks	potential impact on project	stakeholder management actions
CFO	project sponsor	• fully committed to the project, but under severe workload and time pressure • may not always be available for key decisions	high	(a) ....
project leader	leading the project (from purchasing department)	• relatively inexperienced – first major project • fully committed to project goals • solid finance experience	medium	(b) ....
heads of all departments	will operate new system	• will require information and possibly training on new processes and procedures	low	(c) ....
provider of outsourced services	will operate new system	• knows little about the company culture and organisation • may be difficult for them to understand / plan for data bottlenecks in the system	medium	(d) ....
project team members	will execute the project	• may face a lot of negativity from their colleagues in the finance department • may be stressful and cause demotivation, leading to some leaving the project early	medium	(e) ....
employees in finance department	All jobs will change; some will lose their jobs.	• mix of enthusiasm and resistance from this group • those who will lose their jobs may try to sabotage the project	high	(f) ....

3 🎧 **25** Listen to Ayla Demir, project leader, and Pavel Chekov, sponsor, discussing the stakeholder-analysis document, which they have to submit to their board. Note down:
a where they agree
b where the sponsor disagrees, and why
c what actions they decide on.

4 If you were the project's leader or sponsor, what other actions could you take to manage this group of stakeholders effectively?

Focus on language

5 Match these words (a–h), which are often used when discussing staff worries about projects, with their definitions (1–8).

a objection	1 what you show when you are being careful
b reluctant	2 a feeling of anger, often when people are frustrated
c sceptical	3 an argument against something
d caution	4 a kind of enemy
e resentment	5 a worry about something
f opponent	6 unwilling
g concern	7 feeling uninvolved
h disengaged	8 not believing in something

6 The sentences below are recommendations for dealing with stakeholder challenges during a project. Complete them with the correct form of the verbs from the box.

commit	convince	engage	overcome	reassure	strengthen	tackle

a The best way to .... employee concerns about job losses is to state very explicitly that there will be none.

b We need to .... people in the change process by inviting them to participate in workshops which are defining.

c I think that the only way to .... people to change is by explaining very clearly the benefits of the change for them.

d We need to .... any resistance to the project head on. If we don't, we create problems for ourselves later.

e We need to get senior management to .... to the project and persuade their staff to support it.

f I think workshops for affected employees are a good idea to help to .... them that the changes caused by the project are not too enormous.

g We need to .... our marketing message in order to handle any remaining scepticism about the project among key stakeholders.

Let's talk

7 a In groups, look at the project brief on page 90 and prepare a stakeholder analysis which identifies:
  ● the main stakeholders
  ● their stake in the project
  ● possible attitudes/risks of the stakeholders
  ● their possible impact on the project
  ● actions to manage the stakeholders effectively.

b Compare your stakeholder analysis to those produced by other groups. Discuss which you think is the best.

D Intercultural competence: Leading across cultures

1 Think of a leader you admire (now or from history) from the world of sport, politics, economics or science. What qualities does/did this person have which makes/made them a great leader? Are these same qualities important for business leaders? Why?

2 🎧 26 Michaela Wollmann works as Head of Controlling in Insuro, a global insurance company in Switzerland. Christiane McCormack is Head of Sales for Big Buy, a leading electronics retailer in the US. Listen to them discussing leadership. Complete the table below to show how each of them describes the style of leadership in their own organisation. What do they say is the main advantage and disadvantage of each style?

	Insuro	Big Buy
key words		
advantage		
disadvantage		

3 What differences in leadership style have you seen in your organisation/career? What are the advantages and disadvantages of each style? Which do you prefer and why?

4 Look at this list of skills for global business leaders, split into five core areas. Which do you think are the most important? Can you add any further skills which you think are essential for international success?

> **Global perspective**
> • Knows relevant world markets and politics
> • Understands how to balance local and global needs
> • Understands a range of different national cultures
>
> **Organisational capability**
> • Understands how organisations work and sources of potential conflict
> • Can mobilise/influence key stakeholders
> • Represents corporate values across the globe
>
> **Balance of control and flexibility**
> • Focuses on (sustainable) results
> • Defines roles clearly and motivates others with effective rewards
> • Enables people and builds performing teams
>
> **Communication skills across distance**
> • Expresses a clear, inclusive and engaging vision as a leader
> • Opens up fast and frequent two-way communication and listens to different opinions
> • Connects people and know-how in the organisation, using good networking skills
>
> **Personal character**
> • Knows themselves – own thinking style, behaviour and impact on other people
> • Has integrity, tolerance, toughness and creativity – can inspire trust
> • Is flexible enough to use a range of leadership styles

adapted from www.roffeypark.com

5 Compare your ideas with other groups and agree on the single most important skill for leading successfully across cultures.

Case study: Appointing a new project leader

Background Following a sudden resignation at a bank in Madrid last week, a large international branding project needs to appoint a new project leader.

Situation The project started last month, and its objective is to persuade two key markets – the UK and Italy – to rebrand a range of local products, to bring them into line with global branding and promotion. It is clearly understood across the organisation that there will be resistance from local management to this 'centralisation'.

The other members of the project team, mostly from the Spanish headquarters, have been chosen for their expertise in advertising, media management, etc. The team is motivated, but feels overworked.

Task **Work in groups of four. You are a specialist recruitment group from the HR department. You have to recommend a new leader from a list of possible candidates (see below). One of you should chair the meeting.**

Chair: Turn to page 89.
Participant 1:   Turn to page 94.
Participant 2:   Turn to page 96.
Participant 3:   Turn to page 97.

Proposed candidates

David Bexley (aged 42, British)

Experience:	• Been with the company for four years.
	• Previously with a major competitor in UK.
	• Good track record in projects.
Education:	• Arts graduate who went into marketing 15 years ago.
	• Has completed an MBA.
Communication:	• Relatively extrovert, sociable and easy-going with natural abilities to persuade.
	• Speaks only English (quite quickly) and has mainly domestic experience.
	• Noted for his creativity and people skills.

Elio Ronzoni (aged 38, Italian)

Experience:	• Been with the company for 12 years.
	• Worked for six years for an Italian advertising company before being headhunted by the bank.
	• Very creative and knowledgeable about international marketing.
Education:	• Studied Economics and International Marketing in Italy.
Communication:	• Energetic communicator – speaks very quickly.
	• Limited international work experience so far.
	• English skills are intermediate.
	• Seen domestically as a rising star, can work independently.

Lin Ho (aged 34, Singaporean)

Experience:	• Been with the company for eight years.
	• Started as a Marketing Assistant in Singapore.
	• Promoted quickly to Marketing Manager in charge of branding.
	• Worked in Australia for two years, before transferring to Madrid ten months ago.
Education:	• Has an MBA from Stanford University.
	• Is good at getting a job done.
Communication:	• Excellent English and Spanish, as well as her native Chinese.
	• Is learning Italian.
	• Quiet, hard-working and effective.

Gisela Ebke (aged 35, Swiss)

Experience:	• Recruited straight from university.
	• Has been with the bank for 12 years and has a good network among global management.
	• Worked in R&D for six years before accepting an international contract.
	• First posting was to Montreal, Canada. Since then, has been Product Manager for a global brand.
Education:	• Has a PhD in Chemistry.
Communication:	• Speaks Spanish, English and German.
	• Noted for being a very direct and forceful communicator.
	• Very well organised and focuses on achieving results.

E Language reference

Read through the key words and phrases below from this unit. Add any other useful words and expressions which you feel are important for you to learn. Make sure you find the time to review the words and phrases regularly and to use them at work.

People management verbs
offer people rewards/benefits
incentivise
show people recognition
empower (empowerment)
delegate (delegation)
praise
give/get feedback
be a role model for someone
offer people the right terms and conditions
engage/disengage (engagement/disengagement)
motivate/demotivate (motivation/demotivation)

Describing team members
autonomous
creative
easy-going
extroverted
forceful
hard-working
knowledgeable
sociable
well organised

Stakeholder attitudes to projects
convinced (conviction)
reluctant (reluctance)
sceptical (scepticism)
mature (maturity)
cautious (caution)
doubtful (doubt)
certain (certainty)

Culture and leadership
Leadership culture can be:
● entrepreneurial/risk-sensitive
● individualistic/collectivist
● top-down/bottom-up
● formal/informal
● aggressive/caring

Writing task **Choose one of these situations. Try to include at least ten of the project words above in your e-mail.**

1 You are the sponsor of a challenging international project, which is creating a heavy workload for the team. Many of the team members are becoming demotivated due to the pressure involved. Write to the project leader about this situation and recommend some ways to handle the problem.

2 Your manager has just informed you that a large international project is beginning in your part of the organisation next month. The aim is to transfer best practice across similar departments of the organisation in the different countries. Your manager has recommended that you should apply for a leading role in the project. You have been asked to write to the project sponsor, indicating your leadership style, your interest in leading the project and the relevant experience you have.

F Project management tips and personal action plan

1 Take a few minutes to reflect on these project management tips. How far do you agree with each one? Which do you think is most important, and which ideas are most useful?

TIP 1

Make sure you recruit the right people for your team when leading a project – people who have good English, the right skills and with time and motivation to commit to the project.

Idea to help get the right people:

● Discuss nominations to your team with local country managers to ensure you get the right people joining you.

TIP 2

International project work can be demanding and stressful, with lots of work which can be open to supervision from very senior management. Make sure you offer support to your team: emotional support during stress, task support when the job is difficult, and psychological support to maintain motivation.

Ideas to support your team:

● Give praise and positive feedback regularly.
● Find the budget to offer incentives and rewards for a job well done.
● Develop the skills to coach team members.

TIP 3

Take time to create a detailed stakeholder map when planning and managing your project. The challenge with international projects is identifying who the real stakeholders are in the country organisations and what their attitude to your project really is, and understanding how they might be influenced, either by yourself or others.

Ideas to help stakeholder analysis:

● Organise meetings with senior country leaders who may feel that your project is a threat to their authority.
● Use these meetings to clarify the benefits of the project for the local organisation.

Personal action plan

2 Think about what you have learned from this unit. Note down two or three important points which you want to apply to your own job (*What?*). Then create a schedule to implement your learning (*When?*) and think about the best way to check that you have successfully applied the ideas (*How?*).

3 Discuss your personal action plan and adapt it if necessary, based on any useful feedback you get.

	what I learned and want to apply in my projects	when/how I will apply this in my projects	how I will check if I have applied it
1			
2			
3			

Keeping projects on track

AIMS

A To practise monitoring progress and troubleshooting

B To develop effective problem-solving

C To improve the effectiveness of risk management

D To consider different approaches to goal-setting

A Discussion and listening

Think about it

1 In your experience, what kinds of problem can delay a project? Add to this list and discuss which are the most challenging issues.

- Difficulties collecting research data
- Unrealistic deadlines
- People leaving the project team
- Inadequate budgets
- Technology problems
- Unexpected market developments

2 In your experience, what works and what does not work when trying to deal with these problems?

Listen to this

3 🎧 **27–29** **Listen to three international project leaders talking about their experiences of keeping projects on track. Note down the problems which each of them sees as most significant.**

speaker	problems
1 Satoki	
2 Daniel	
3 Anna	

4 Read this e-mail from a team member to his leader about a delay to their project. As project leader, how would you feel if you received this e-mail?

> Dear Sandy
> I'm afraid that we will be unable to complete the software upgrade next week on time. We have run into some problems which we didn't expect. However, I'm sure we will be able to get everything done by the end of the month – so no more than an eight-day delay.
> If you would like a call to discuss this, do let me know and we can schedule something.
> Regards, Pavel

5 🎧 **30–32** Listen to the project leaders from Exercise 3 discussing their reactions to the e-mail in Exercise 4. In which ways do they think the same as / differently to you? After listening to their opinions about the e-mail, which project leader do you most agree with, and why?

Focus on language **6** Choose the correct option to complete each of these comments about the progress of projects.

    a Things have gone really well. We should be able to finish everything *on / in* time.

    b We haven't finished all the tasks *yet / still* in Phase 1. We need another week.

    c The project leader is very happy with the speed of our work. We're already around two weeks *before / ahead of* schedule.

    d We're waiting for the IT department to install the new software. *Already / In the meantime*, we'll start to train users.

    e Things have gone a little too slowly. We need to speed up if we're going to finish *until / by* our deadline of the end of this month.

    f We're under pressure, so we need to move to the next phase of the project *meanwhile / shortly*.

    g *As of today / Current*, we have spent approximately $2m on the project.

7 a Complete the sentences below describing changes to a project schedule using the verbs from the box.

amend	bring forward	ditch	integrate	postpone
replace	reprioritise	revisit	swap	tighten up

    a We have fallen behind schedule, so we need to .... the deadline to the end of May. If you agree, I will .... the project schedule and send a new version to all team members.

    b We need to look again at quality levels, which I think are too low. We really have to .... here.

    c There are too many tasks at the moment, and it's causing stress for everyone. I suggest we .... and .... those which are least important.

    d Peter and Luis are not in the right roles for this project. I suggest we .... them around, as they are better suited to doing each other's tasks.

    e Can we .... budgets at the next project meeting, as I'm worried we are going to overspend.

    f Would it be possible to .... the product testing from next month to this?

    g Martine has just told me she will be leaving the company, so we will need to .... her at the end of this month.

    h The company is going to announce a new growth strategy for next year. Can we .... this message somehow into the project communication package?

b With a partner, use the verbs from the box to describe your own working schedule and changes to plans at work. Try to use each of the verbs at least once.

Let's talk **8** Work in pairs. You are team members of an international construction project. The project leader needs to phone the sponsor to update on some problems in the project and agree a new schedule.

Student A (project leader):   Turn to page 90.
Student B (project sponsor): Turn to page 95.

Prepare and then role-play the telephone conversation. You should agree and both note down changes to your project schedules as you speak. After the call, compare your schedules and see if you have the same information and timelines on your schedules.

Think about it **1** One important purpose of project team meetings is to discuss and solve problems. Look at what Martha Perez, an international project leader from Colombia, says about her experience of such meetings. What are your experiences of international meetings? Do you agree with Martha's ideas about what makes these kinds of meetings effective?

> Most of the project meetings to discuss problems are very ineffective. People don't listen – they argue and then defend their own ideas and solutions. The same people do most of the talking, usually the native English speakers who have a natural language advantage. Not enough effort is given to finding creative solutions, which will work across all the different countries involved in the project. For me, the most important thing in these kinds of challenging meetings is a strong chairperson, with a clear structure and agenda, and participants who can communicate respectfully with each other.

Listen to this **2** 🎧 **33** Listen to part of a meeting. The chair uses a structured approach to begin the meeting. Complete these notes he has prepared.

> **Project meeting**
>
> 1 Say a quick word of **(a)** ....
> 2 Mention Fiona and **(b)** ....
> 3 Run over agenda items:
>   • briefing from me about **(c)** ....
>   • **(d)** .... updates
>   • input about **(e)** .... from Klaus
>   • focus on **(f)** .... as a major discussion topic

3 🎧 **34** Listen to a later part of the same meeting and answer these questions.

   a What simple question does the chair ask at the beginning to invite ideas and get the discussion going?
   b How does he handle the interruption from Pedro?
   c What does he do to make the group reflect on Katarina's ideas? What is the result of this?
   d How well do you think the chair handled the interruptions and strong disagreements in this part of the meeting? Why?

4 How well do you think the chair handled the interruption from Pedro and the meeting in general?

5 Look at this list of communication skills and phrases for leading and participating in meetings in English. Complete the short phrases with a word / words of your own and compare your answers to those on page 91. Then brainstorm other phrases you might use in the same situations.

Opening

Signal that it is time to start	*Let's (**a**) .... started.*
Welcome and apologise for any absences	*Apologies from Fiona. She's ...*
Confirm if agenda/documents received	*Do you all have a (**b**) .... of the agenda?*
Introduce the agenda and objectives	*As you can see from the agenda, ...*

Handling the discussion

Ask for opinions	*What do you think about this, Jean?*
Give opinions	*My (**c**) .... is that we need to ...*
Clarify what was said	*Sorry, did you mean that ... ?*
Prevent interruptions	*Please let Michel finish. Then I'll (**d**) .... to you.*
Focus the meeting on key points	*Can we come back to the (**e**) .... issue here?*

Closing

Move the meeting to a decision	*I think we need to make a decision.*
Summarise action points	*So, to (**f**) .... up, we have decided to ...*
Check if any remaining questions	*Are there any questions?*
Promise to send minutes	*I'll get the minutes to you (**g**) .... the end of today.*
Confirm next meeting	*So, the next meeting is ...*
Thank and end	*Thanks everyone. Let's (**h**) .... there.*

6 Sometimes it is necessary to handle quite challenging people in meetings. Look at the types of people below and a possible way of responding to them. Compare your answers to those in the key (page 116). Can you think of other types of communicator and strategies for handling them? Look at page 91 for some ideas.

Someone who argues
I think your comments are rather negative, Mike. What do *you* think is the best way forward?

Someone who is shy
Isabella, what's your view?

Somone who complains
Matthieu, I know you are unhappy, but let's try to find a solution.

Someone who talks a lot
Brian, do you think we could discuss this in detail later?

7 You are part of the project management team at the headquarters of your company. You are asked to meet from time to time to discuss general issues relating to project management in the company.

- Look at the agenda on page 91 and prepare your ideas.
- Meet in small groups, appoint a chairperson and discuss the three points. Make a note of your decisions to discuss briefly with the other groups.
- At the end of your meeting, give feedback to each other on how well you think the meeting went.

Think about it 1 If risks are not managed effectively in projects, failure is more likely. Make a list of possible risks, then compare them with the list on page 98. Can you add to them? In your experience, which are most significant? Why?

2 What methods have you used to manage risk in projects in the past? What worked well? What did not work well? Why?

Read this 3 Read the article below on managing risk in projects and match each of these rules (a–j) to the correct paragraph (1–10).

a Communicate about risks	**f** Analyse risks
b Prioritise risks	**g** Track risks
c Clarify ownership issues	**h** Identify risks early in your project
d Register project risks	**i** Plan and implement risk responses
e Consider threats and opportunities	**j** Make risk mangement part of your project

Ten golden rules of project risk management
by Bart Jutte

The benefits of risk management in dealing with the uncertainties and complexities of international projects are huge. This article gives you the ten golden rules to apply risk management successfully in your project.

1 *Make risk management part of your project*

Integrate professional risk management as soon as you can into your project, so you can get the full benefits of this approach. Smart project managers provide training in risk management to the team from the beginning.

2 ....

Team sessions are the common method to brainstorm the risks people know. Take advantage of the personal experience and expertise of team members. Talk to experts outside the project with the right track record. They can help you to find hidden dangers you might meet or golden opportunities that may not have crossed your mind.

3 ....

Reports on failed projects show that the project managers were frequently unaware of problems about to hit them. The frightening finding is that frequently someone in the project organisation actually did see the problem, but didn't inform the project manager. Communicate frequently in team meetings by making project risks part of the agenda.

4 ....

The word *risk* has a negative feeling. However, modern risk management also focuses on positive risks, the project opportunities. These are the unplanned events that can benefit your project and organisation. These can make your project faster, better and more profitable.

5 ....

Some project managers think they are finished once they have created a list of risks. However, this is only a starting point. The next step is to make clear who is responsible for which risk. Someone has to take responsibility, otherwise the risk is not taken care of properly.

6 ....

A project manager once told me, 'I treat all risks equally.' This makes project life really simple. However, it doesn't deliver the best possible results. Some risks have a higher impact than others. Check if you have any 'showstoppers' in your project that could crash your project. If so, these are your number-one priority.

7 ....

Risk analysis involves understanding two dimensions: the causes and the potential impacts of a risk event. The first thing to do is to list the circumstances that decrease or increase the chance of a risk happening in the first place. Understanding the consequences of a risk means mapping what would happen if the risk became reality.

8 ....

When dealing with threats, you have three options: avoidance, minimisation and acceptance. Avoiding risks means you organise your project so you don't encounter a risk any more, e.g. changing a supplier. Interestingly, acceptance can be a good choice if the effects on the project are minimal or the possibilities to influence it prove to be very difficult, time-consuming or relatively expensive.

9 ....

Maintaining a risk log helps you to view progress and make sure that you don't forget about risk. A good log contains risks descriptions and clarifies ownership issues.

10 ....

Tracking risks focuses on the current situation of risks. Which are more likely to happen? Has the relative importance of risks changed? Answering these questions will help to pay attention to the risks that matter most for your project.

adapted from *www.projectsmart.co.uk*

4 a Read the article again and answer these questions.

    a Who can help the project manager to discover project risks?

    b What is the 'frightening finding' from reports on failed projects, and the lesson for project managers?

    c What is a 'showstopper', and what is the recommended way to handle such a thing?

    d When can it be acceptable to simply accept a risk and do nothing about it?

    e What is the value of a risk log?

b Which of the ideas in the article do you most/least agree with? Why?

Focus on language **5 a Complete the extract below from a presentation by a project leader at a kick-off meeting using the words from the box.**

eliminate	exposed	log	mitigate	predict
put in place	seek	tackle	tolerate	track

Let me just turn briefly to the important issue of risk. I think as a team we need to work very hard in this project to **(a)** .... head on any major risks which could derail the project. What I want to pilot is some risk management, which will allow us to **(b)** .... future problems and to **(c)** .... some effective contingency plans, which will **(d)** .... the worst potential effects. The software also allows us to **(e)** .... risks in an Excel template, and then we can **(f)** .... things closely with a regular focus in our team meetings. We won't **(g)** .... risks completely, but it means we are not **(h)** .... to potentially dangerous levels of risk. Of course, there will be cases where we simply have to **(i)** .... risks – for cost reasons, perhaps. In such cases, I'm aiming to **(j)** .... approval from the sponsor for any decision we make before we proceed.

b 🎧 **35** **Listen to the presentation and check your answers.**

6 Look at two examples of a way in which it is possible to discuss risk – first by highlighting it, then by analysing the consequences and then by proposing action. Work in pairs and apply this three-stage process to the project risks below (a–d). See how many different consequences and actions you can suggest for each risk.

	highlight the risk	analyse consequences	propose action
1	There could be legal issues behind this which we don't know about.	If this is the case, we may have to slow the project down.	What about contacting the legal department for some advice?
2	We may not have enough money to deliver this. I think we're underestimating the cost.	This could destabilise/ undermine the whole project.	I think we have to insist on more funding.

    a There's a real risk that some of these stakeholders will not accept the project leader.

    b Is there a possibility that the company could post a loss at the end of the year?

    c What if the technology fails to deliver on its promises?

    d I think there are dangers in relying too much on teleconferences in the project.

Let's talk **7 Your international company wants to increase the use of e-learning in the company over the next two years for all training, from language to leadership. This will deliver huge savings by reducing travel and classroom training costs and will help to standardise the training curriculum in different countries.**
In groups, discuss the risks of such a project. Think about the possible actions which should be considered by the project team to manage these risks.

D Intercultural competence: Focusing on goals

1 Work in pairs to discuss these attitudes to goals in projects. Which do you agree/disagree with? Why?

> Successful project leaders need to be very goal-focused. Setting and reaching goals are fundamentals of project management.

> One of the main differences with international projects is that goals need to become flexible, because things are changing all the time.

> Being goal-oriented is not enough for success in projects. People-focus is more important.

> Reaching team goals is more important than reaching personal goals in international projects.

> Setting individual goals for team members is important to motivate performance in a team.

> Leaders have to decide what 'goal' means – is it achieving the deadline or achieving the right quality solution? Very often, both are not possible in projects.

2 🎧 **36–37** **Michelle Legeaux works for GFR, an energy company based in Paris. She is leading a project to modernise a gas power station in the south of France. Georgy Dorokhov is one of many external technical consultants who have been recruited to support the project. Listen and answer these questions.**

a What does Michelle describe as the main goal of the project?

b How does Michelle describe the working style of the external consultants? Why is this a problem for the project?

c What conflict does Michelle describe?

d What mistakes does Georgy see with the project leadership?

e What does Georgy do to get decisions quickly in the project?

3 What do you think is the best way for those running international projects to deal with such problems?

4 Some cultures are described as being typically 'high goal focus', meaning that goals are given a very high priority. Others are described as 'low goal focus', which means that other considerations are often given more emphasis. Complete the summary below, using words from the box.

direction	flexible	local	original	resistance	waste	willing

high goal focus	low goal focus
potential advantages • More likely to achieve **(a)** .... objectives. • Can give a strong sense of **(b)** .... for others. • Keeps things clear and simple most of the time.	**potential advantages** • **(d)** .... to adapt to local ways and priorities. • Can explore different opportunities. • Can operate in a **(e)** .... and customer-friendly way.
potential disadvantages • May overlook changing circumstances. • May compromise relationship-building. • May create **(c)** .... and conflict in local business units.	**potential disadvantages** • Easily distracted from the main task. • May **(f)** .... time and money. • May be too influenced by **(g)** .... considerations.

5 Think about your own international working style in terms of goal focus. Are you high, low or somewhere in between the two? Think about your style in a range of possible international project contexts. Note down three things you should do in order to manage goals effectively. Compare your ideas with others in the class.

Case study: A question of goals

Background

Csaba Grozer is a research-and-development scientist working for MedTech, a manufacturer of high-quality surgery equipment based in Budapest, Hungary.

He is leading a project to develop new lasers for eye surgery. The project is part of a larger programme of laser-based development, which is co-ordinated from the company's office in London.

The programme manager and project sponsor is Michaela Arens, a senior executive based in London, who travels extensively in order to manage the full project programme for the company.

Situation

Csaba is worried that a number of technical problems will soon put his project schedule under pressure. He urgently needs to talk to Michaela in order to get approval to employ extra technicians, required to solve the problems and avoid future delay. No meeting has yet been organised, due to Michaela's constant travelling. Telephone conferences are also cancelled regularly. E-mail is the only realistic channel of communication.

Csaba's project does not seem to be a priority for Michaela. This is a real issue for Csaba, as he hates to miss any targets or deadlines. He decides to e-mail Michaela to try to deal with the situation.

> Dear Michaela
> As per my previous e-mails, I am concerned about a number of technical issues which are threatening to cause delays to the eye-surgery project.
> I would like to schedule an urgent meeting – possibly in London – to discuss the status of this project. I think it would also be useful to discuss how we can communicate together effectively in the future, to keep things on track and avoid unnecessary delays.
> I look forward to hearing from you.
> Regards, Csaba

Michaela schedules a telephone conference with Csaba after receiving his e-mail. However, she cancels that meeting later in the day, as she has to go on an urgent business trip. No new appointment is scheduled.

Task

1 **In small groups, discuss these questions.**

   a How much do you sympathise with Csaba's frustration?

   b How do you think Michaela sees the situation?

   c How useful was Csaba's e-mail?

2 **Write a second e-mail which Csaba could send to Michaela to help to resolve the situation. You can invent any necessary information.**

Read through the key words and phrases below from this unit. Add any other useful words and expressions which you feel are important for you to learn. Make sure you find the time to review the words and phrases regularly and to use them at work.

Project schedule verbs

postpone	bring forward
delay	amend
replace	reprioritise
ditch	swap
revisit	integrate

Deadlines

Verbs	*Nouns*
meet	an unrealistic deadline
respect	a tight deadline
miss	a milestone
fail to meet	a sub-milestone
ignore	

Time expressions

on time	We finished everything *on time* and according to schedule.
in time (to)	We finished the meeting *in time to* have a final cup of coffee before driving to the airport.
as of today	*As of today*, we have 33 people working in the project.
yet	I haven't finished the report *yet*. Have you finished the report *yet*?
still	No, I'm *still* working on the report.
for the time being	Let's wait *for the time being* and see what happens.
indefinitely	We postponed construction *indefinitely*. We have no idea when we will restart.
in the meantime	OK, I'll wait for you to send me the report. *In the meantime*, I'll talk to Alan about his ideas for management training.
already	What do you mean, 'When will I finish the report?'? I've *already* finished it – I e-mailed it to you yesterday. Didn't you receive it?
ahead of schedule	Great news! We are *ahead of schedule*.
on schedule	Everything is fine. We are *on schedule* and on budget.
behind schedule	We are *behind schedule*. In fact, we're three days late.
by	I need your report *by* Friday at the latest.
until	I'll be in the office *until* seven o'clock. Then I'll go home.
shortly	See you *shortly*. (= soon)

Writing task **Choose one of these situations. Try to include at least ten of the project words above in your e-mail.**

1 Write an e-mail which outlines the status of a project you are involved in. You should describe which tasks/milestones have been completed/reached, give details of any delays or problems in the project which exist and make recommendations to keep the project on track in the short/medium term.

2 Write a short risk report on a project in which you are / will be involved. Describe the main risks, the potential consequences of the risks and propose actions to deal with the risks – either to avoid, minimise or accept.

F Project management tips and personal action plan

1 Take a few minutes to reflect on these project management tips. How far do you agree with each one? Which do you think is most important, and which ideas are most useful?

TIP 1

Be aware that a lack of communication is a major risk to a project. It is vital to dedicate resources in your project team to manage both internal and external communication.
Idea to help communication:
- Take time to plan face-to-face meetings in detail. Run feedback sessions with the project team on communication in the project – in meetings, by e-mail and with external stakeholders.

TIP 2

Make risk management a strategic part of your project. Project management as a discipline has been poor at risk management historically. Yet the risks involved in international projects can be unexpected and very serious.
Idea to help risk management:
- Get advice from experts in risk management in your organisation on how to manage project risk professionally.

TIP 3

Make sure everyone in your project has a common understanding and approach to goals. If this is unclear, it is easy for conflict to arise in the team.
Idea to help understanding:
- Schedule a meeting early in the project to clarify attitudes to goals, deadlines, quality and schedules by discussing a number of questions, e.g. How important is it to reach our goals on time?, Is it possible to miss a deadline?, How do we measure quality?, What is *acceptable quality?*, etc.

Personal action plan 2 Think about what you have learned from this unit. Note down two or three important points which you want to apply to your own job (*What?*). Then create a schedule to implement your learning (*When?*) and think about the best way to check that you have successfully applied the ideas (*How?*).

3 Discuss your personal action plan and adapt it if necessary, based on any useful feedback you get.

	what I learned and want to apply in my projects	when/how I will apply this in my projects	how I will check if I have applied it
1			
2			
3			

5 Building better communication

AIMS

A To understand communication challenges in projects
B To practise managing teleconferences
C To develop feedback skills
D To improve personal communication style

A Discussion and listening

Think about it

1 Think of someone at work who you think is an effective communicator. Make a list of the things that they do which make them effective. Which thing is most important? Why?

2 How can project leaders ensure that team members communicate effectively with each other?

Listen to this

3 🎧 **38** Roberto Rodríguez, Nisha Sharma and Anne-Marie Thoral all work for Unibrand, one of the world's leading food companies. Last year, they worked together as members of an international project, which successfully created a cross-border advertising campaign for the company's pizza range. Listen to the team describing problems with communication they experienced during the project and answer these questions.

a Which communication problem does Roberto describe?

b What possible reasons does he give for the problem?

c What problems with documentation did Nisha experience?

d What does Anne-Marie describe as 'frustrating'?

e What were the reasons for this problem?

4 🎧 **39** At the end of the discussion in Exercise 3, the team mentioned that communication improved when a new project leader came on board. What do you think the leader did to solve the problems which they described? Listen to the rest of the discussion and compare your answers to the solutions they describe.

5 Which of the ideas discussed by Roberto, Nisha and Anne-Marie would be most useful for your own project teams? Why? Which idea(s) would not work? Why?

Focus on language **6** Roberto talked about the importance of asking questions. Look at these three types of questions: open, clarification and check. Which do you think is easiest / most difficult to ask? Why?

open questions	clarification questions	check questions
Which/Why is ...? What/When are we ...? When/Who do you ...?	What do you mean by 'urgent'? Interesting, why do you say 'It's impossible'? When you say 'soon', do you mean that ...?	So you think that ... For you, it's important to ... So this means we can ...

7 a 🎧 **40** Sam Stone is based in New York and leads a project with team members Padma Chopra in India and Marco Branco in Mexico. Listen to an extract from a recent teleconference, discussing the project schedule, and answer these questions.

   a Which open question is used to start the discussion?

   b Which information is clarified first by the project leader?

   c What question does she ask to clarify a second time? Why does she think it is necessary to clarify again?

   d Which check question does she use to confirm the situation?

   b What do you think about Marco's communication style? How common is this type of behaviour in your experience? How well do you think the project leader handled him? Why?

8 Look at these statements made by team members to their leader in project update meetings. As the team leader, write down different questions you might ask to clarify what is being said, choosing from the three questions types in Exercise 6. Then compare your answers to those on pages 117–118.

   a 'I need some more time to finish this report.'

   b 'We have a few resource problems in my region.'

   c 'I think there are advantages to delaying the project.'

   d 'In my opinion, we have no option but to raise this problem with the sponsor.'

   e 'I think that most of this data is simply unreliable.'

Let's talk **9 a** You are about to join a new international project. At the beginning of the project, the leader wants to create an online 'team book' with personal profiles of all the team members. Working in pairs, interview each other and note down information which you could include in a profile. Take a few minutes to plan a few open questions under each heading.

   ● My main responsibilities are ...

   ● The most difficult thing about my job is ...

   ● When communicating, I think it's important for teams to ...

   ● Never write e-mails which ...

   ● Good teamwork is all about ...

   ● My main passions outside work are ...

   b When you have interviewed each other, discuss which questions worked well, and why.

B Communication skills: Teleconferencing

Think about it   **1 What is your experience of teleconferencing, either leading it or participating in it? What do you think are the extra challenges of communicating in this kind of meeting?**

2 What tips would you give to those leading or participating in teleconference calls to make communication effective?

Listen to this   **3 🎧 41 Listen to the start of a teleconference call and answer these questions.**

    a What topic does the chair use for small talk as participants log into the call?

    b What does the chair ask the new team member to do? Why?

    c What does the new team member promise to do after the call? Why does he do this *after* the meeting?

    d Which communication rules does the chair encourage the participants to respect during the conference call?

4 🎧 42 Listen to a later extract of the same meeting and answer these questions.

    a Why does the chair involve Tomás in the discussion?

    b How does the chair handle the technical problem with sound during the meeting?

    c What does the chair promise to do as Julia leaves the meeting?

5 What do you like about the way the chair handled this telephone conference? Why?

Focus on language   **6 With a partner, brainstorm what a chair should do to manage the specific problems of a teleconference call, and actual phrases which could be used. Use the ideas below as a starting point. You can also look at the audio scripts of the meeting you listened to on page 107 to get more ideas. Compare your ideas with those on page 118.**

chairing a conference call	example phrases
as people enter the call Check identity of people.	*Is that John?*
at the start of the discussion Give some basic rules for the conference call.	*Please confirm your agreement by saying something.*
during the discussion Ask people by name to say something.	*Lars, what do you think about this?*
at the end of the call Re-confirm actions.	*Let me go over that we have agreed just to be clear. We have decided to ...*

5 Building better communication

7 Complete the checklist of phrases below for participants of conference calls using the words from the box.

| add | come | dial | got | hand | make | see | stop |

interrupting

a Sorry to interrupt. It's Bob in London here. Can I just .... something?

b Peter, sorry. I need to .... in here for a second, because that's not correct.

handling an interruption

c Paul, can I finish this point and then I'll .... over? Thanks.

d Julia, just one more thing on this and then I'll ....

presenting information

e Can everyone .... the slide?

f Have you all .... page 11 on the screen?

reporting a technical problem

g The reception is very bad. I'm going to .... in again. OK?

h The slide isn't displaying properly. I can't .... it out.

8 Brainstorm other technical problems which might happen in a conference call and what you could say to deal with the situation.

Let's talk **9** Work in groups. You work for the Project Management Office of your organisation and are based in different international locations in the organisation. You hold regular teleconferences, with the objective of finding ways to improve efficiency and quality across all projects.

Read the e-mail below from your CEO, which asks for recommendations to solve a specific problem in your organisation's projects. After reading the e-mail, appoint one person to chair a teleconference to discuss the problem. If you are the chair, take a few minutes to prepare how to run the meeting. If you are a participant, you should prepare by reading your role card on page 96.

Remember, it is a telephone meeting so no one is able to see each other. To simulate this, sit in a small circle with everyone facing outwards.

To: PMO
From: CEO
Subject: English language

During recent meetings with heads of large projects across the organisation, I was made aware of a significant communication issue limiting the efficiency of our work. Many non-native English speakers complain that native English speakers, particularly from the UK and the US, are speaking too quickly and using too many complex words during teleconferences.

All this makes it very difficult to understand them, and it is generating a lot of resentment.

Many feel the native speakers are using their language as a weapon to dominate and influence decisions.

The Board would like a set of creative recommendations from you by the end of next week on how we should tackle this problem, so please discuss this at your next PMO meeting and come up with some ideas to solve this issue.

Best regards
CEO

After the meeting, discuss how it went and list things which went well and things which could be improved next time.

Think about it **1 Work in pairs. Discuss your experience of feedback at work using these questions.**

person Which people do you like to give feedback to / get feedback from? (manager, colleagues, customers, etc.)

purpose What is the objective of feedback which you give/get? (praise, criticism, etc.)

place Where/How does the feedback happen? (team meeting, individual meeting, by e-mail, etc.)

emotions How do you usually react to positive/negative feedback?

2 What is the most useful feedback (positive or negative) that you have had in your career so far?

Read this **3 Read the article below on giving feedback and answer these questions.**

a What benefits can teams get from greater use of feedback?

b What is the best way to start a feedback conversation?

c What should you never do in a feedback session?

d How can questions be useful when giving feedback?

e How do people often react when getting feedback? What are the consequences of reacting in this way?

Creating a feedback culture in the team

Most project teams would agree that developing a strong feedback culture is useful. Feedback can create greater openness, facilitate team learning and help teams to find ways to work together more efficiently. However, feedback means different things in different places. For some, no feedback means that you did a good job. In other cultures, lots of positive feedback is not only effective but expected! So what kind of feedback style might work in a project team with many different cultures? Here are some tips to help your own teams.

TIP 1 Feedback should begin with positives – saying what people have done well. This creates a good atmosphere and opens up people to accepting constructive criticism later: *Let's start with what has gone well …*

TIP 2 When giving more critical feedback on others' behaviour, it's important to describe behaviour in a totally neutral way, e.g. *You walked into the meeting and sat down without shaking hands,* and to explain the consequences of this behaviour on others, e.g. *Some people felt this was a little rude.* Never evaluate a person's behaviour negatively – e.g. *You were rude yesterday* – from your own point of view or criticise someone's personality, e.g. *You're rude.*

TIP 3 Feedback should be a constructive, two-way process, and will always involve different perceptions of events. So it's important to use questions such as *What do you think about this feedback? Did you know that others felt this way about your behaviour?* or *What could you do differently?* Questions like these help to encourage the recipient to think about the consequences of their behaviour.

TIP 4 At the end of a formal feedback session, the recipient should, ideally, agree to do something differently to have a more positive impact, e.g. *OK, I will try to come across as more open and polite by …*

TIP 5 When receiving feedback, people often react defensively and say things like *That's not true* or *Yes, but …* Yet for the recipient, whether the feedback is accurate or not, it is always useful information on how others see you, and it can provide great information to help you lead and co-operate more effectively, e.g. *So do you think that if I do … then we can …?* If you're not open to how others see you, you'll be slower to learn ways to improve your performance and to create a better team spirit.

adapted from *Communicating across cultures* (B. Dignen, CUP)

4 Which tips in the article do you agree most with? Why? How could your own team or department improve the way it uses feedback as a tool to develop performance?

5 Look at the conversation below in which Pilar, a project leader, gives feedback to Will, a team member, about his communication style with a colleague in Italy. Complete the conversation using these questions.

Is there another way to do things?	Do you remember writing that?
What do you think about this?	Can you see the impact it's having on the team?
When can you organise a meeting?	Can I talk to you for a second?

Pilar: Will? **(a)** .... I just had a call from Franco in Milan.

Will: Oh, Franco. You know he's late again with his part of the project? I don't know what the problem is. I just e-mailed him about it.

Pilar: He was telling me about some of your e-mails. They are coming across as very direct and even rude. **(b)** ....

Will: I'm not rude.

Pilar: I think that to Franco they feel rude. In your last e-mail, I saw that you actually wrote: 'The Milan office is inefficient.' **(c)** ....

Will: Yes, I do. But the Milan office *is* inefficient!

Pilar: But think about this, Will. **(d)** .... It's beginning to damage the way we work together. **(e)** .... This is causing conflict for everyone.

Will: I'm in Milan next week. I can organise a meeting to talk about this.

Pilar: Remember, Franco's under a lot of pressure, at home as well as work. **(f)** ....

Will: I'll e-mail him this afternoon. Thanks, Pilar. That was useful.

6 In the left-hand column of the chart below is a 12-step process for giving feedback. A project leader is worried because, at a recent presentation, some senior managers felt criticised by a team member who suggested that they were not supporting the project. Work in pairs to complete what the project leader said to the team member in the right-hand column, following the process and using your own words.

1 Organise a feedback meeting	Can we have a .... ?
2 Begin the meeting with a clear objective	I'd like to give you some feedback ....
3 Begin by asking questions about the situation	How did you feel .... ?
4 Start with positive comments	I think your talk was well organised and ....
5 Describe behaviour	You said at the beginning of the meeting ....
6 Present the situation from other points of view	I think the senior managers were ....
7 Ask for a response	What do you think .... ?
8 Explore alternative behaviour	How could you have .... ?
9 Comment on the person's ideas	I think that sounds like ....
10 Propose more ideas for alternative behaviour	I think another thing you could do ....
11 Summarise	So, just to summarise, how will you .... ?
12 Get feedback on your feedback	How useful .... ?

Let's talk **7** Work in pairs to create your own feedback scenario. Prepare a similar conversation between a project leader and a team member. Here are some ideas to help you.

- The team member has missed a number of important deadlines recently.
- The quality of the team member's work has fallen in recent months.
- The team member is not contributing much in team meetings.
- Other team members have complained that the person is taking a long time (up to two weeks) to reply to e-mails.

D Intercultural competence: Communication styles

1 Some experts have analysed the differences in communication style in various cultures. For example, in his book *Understanding American and German business cultures*, Patrick Schmidt contrasts the two cultures and their general styles of communication. Remember, he is describing cultures and not individuals.

German	American
complex	simple
thoughtful	fast
detailed	concise
formal	informal
reserved	personal

How useful/accurate do you think this analysis is? Which words would you use to describe the communication style of other cultures you know?

2 🎧 43–45 Listen to three professionals from different projects describing the communication culture of their teams. Make a note of the main features of each team culture.

3 Read the article below, then answer these questions. Take time to complete the personal profile in the article as you read through.

a Why is it useful to take time to profile our own communication style?

b Which is more important to understand our style – personality or culture?

c What is the reason for finishing by listing personal strengths and weaknesses?

—— What is your communication style? ——
50 ways to improve your intercultural skills

Generalisations or stereotypes at the level of national culture can provide an interesting if dangerous platform for reflection and discussion. However, it is more important to understand our own personal style, because it can help us to understand how we come across to our international partners – how clear we are, how direct we are, how polite or impolite we may seem.

As individuals, we each have a personal communication style. We communicate the *what* and the *why* in different ways for both psychological – we may be extroverted or introverted – and cultural reasons – we may be direct or indirect. Both personality and culture can be equally important. These different styles affect the clarity and impact of our communication for those listening to us.

Here is a quick and informal personal profiling process using the following checklist. To complete your profile, simply circle the word in each of the pairs below which most correctly describes your personal style. Note down any other words which you think are important to describe how you communicate. Finish by writing what you see as the strengths and possible risks of your style when communicating internationally.

complex	simple
thoughtful	fast
detailed	concise
formal	informal
reserved	personal

strengths of my communication style	risks of my communication style

4 Ask a partner if they agree with your profile.

5 Decide which aspects of your communication style you may need to adapt, and how you can adapt.

Case study: Developing effective team communication

Background Patricia works for an international telecoms company, which operates in Europe and South America. She is leading an international project, part of which involves managing the integration of a successful research-and-development company, Teltech, recently acquired by her company. One member of her project team, Janek Ivanov, is from Teltech, and was appointed to support the integration process in any way possible.

Situation Patricia is becoming increasingly frustrated with Janek. He is very passive in meetings and says very little, which makes it difficult to really know if he agrees with or even understands what is said. He is rarely creative and spends most of his time criticising weaknesses in others' ideas. Patricia decides not to discuss the issue directly with Janek, because she does not think the discussion will be useful. Instead, she phones Sarah Miller, Janek's boss in Teltech, to discuss the problem.

Tasks

1 Discuss these questions.
  a What do you think could be the main issues here?
  b What do you think of Patricia's decision to phone Sarah? What other options are there for dealing with this situation? Which do you think is the best/worst?

2 🎧 46 Patricia has e-mailed Sarah to explain the situation. Listen to the phone call they now have.
  a Which two possible reasons does Sarah give to explain the situation?
  b What does Patricia decide to do next?

3 Discuss these questions.
  a How far do you think Sarah's explanations could be correct?
  b What do you think of Patricia's next step? What do you think will happen?

4 🎧 47 Listen to the discussion between Patricia and Janek.
  a What main reason does Janek give for his communication style in team meetings?
  b What does Patricia say she's going to do next?

5 Discuss Patricia's handling of this conversation. What is the problem here? How does she decide to handle it? What else could she do to deal with this issue?

6 Generally, how well do you think Patricia handled this situation? Agree a score from 1 to 10 (10 is high) and explain the reasons for your score to other groups.

7 With a partner, add to the list of strategies below for dealing with quieter participants during a meeting. Decide on one which you prefer most, then explain your strategy to the rest of the class.

  Strategies for dealing with quieter participants
  ● Encourage them before the meeting to say more.
  ● Involve the person directly by saying something like 'What do you think, Naomi?'

Read through the key words and phrases below from this unit. Add any other useful words and expressions which you feel are important for you to learn. Make sure you find the time to review the words and phrases regularly and to use them at work.

Communication media
a virtual meeting
a conference call
a teleconference
an audio/video conference

Communication verbs
argue
criticise
evaluate
praise
facilitate
chair
participate in
dial in
log in
hand over

Communication styles

complex	simple
thoughtful	fast
detailed	concise
formal	informal
reserved	personal
introverted	extroverted

Writing task **Choose one of these situations. Try to include at least ten of the project words above in your e-mail.**

1 You are working on an international project in which many Australians and South Africans are participating. Many of your non-native English-speaking colleagues have started to complain that they cannot understand the native speakers during conference calls. They are beginning to become a little resentful and demotivated by this situation. Write an e-mail to the project leader describing the problem and including one or two suggestions on how to improve the situation.

2 Your project leader wants to publish short biographies of all members of her international project on a special team intranet site. She has requested everyone (including you) to send a 200-word description of themselves (professional and personal information) as soon as possible. Send the information in an e-mail with your feedback on the idea – if you think it is good or bad, and why.

F Project management tips and personal action plan

1 Take a few minutes to reflect on these project management tips. How far do you agree with each one? Which do you think is most important, and which ideas are most useful? Remember, these are only ideas and you need to think about which are relevant and can be applied in your own project environment.

TIP 1

Telephone conference calls (teleconferences) are rapidly becoming a key communication channel for international project teams. It is important that the person leading your virtual meetings is a competent facilitator and can use the techniques featured in this unit. Additionally, participants must understand their responsibility to interrupt if they do not understand and to participate fully when required to contribute ideas.

Idea to support your team:
● Run a regular feedback session at the end of your conference calls and discuss if there are any ways in which the team can improve its use of this communication channel.

TIP 2

Build an open and constructive feedback culture into your project team early. Feedback is a mechanism to allow individuals to understand each others' needs and to learn how to co-operate effectively. The challenge is that feedback is practised differently across business cultures.

Idea to support your team:
● Discuss expectations and styles of feedback explicitly in the team and agree a feedback process together which everyone can commit to.

TIP 3

Know your own communication style. Know what is likely to work with some people and irritate others. Try to maximise your strengths and minimise any weaknesses which may damage communication in the team.

Idea to support your team:
● Use some form of profiling tool and a formal feedback session to develop your approach. Ideally, the team should do this as a team-building exercise.

Personal action plan 2 Take 15 minutes to review the unit. Note down at least three important points you have learned and that you want to apply to your own projects. Then commit to a schedule to implement your learning and think about how you can check if you have been successful, e.g. ask for feedback.

	what I learned and want to apply in my projects	when/how I will apply this in my projects	how I will check if I have applied it
1			
2			
3			

6 Dealing with conflict

AIMS

A To understand how to avoid conflict
B To develop negotiation skills
C To manage conflict by e-mail
D To define rules for team behaviour

— **A Discussion and listening** —

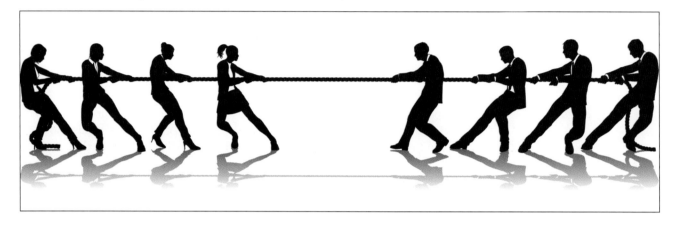

Think about it   **1** How would you describe the difference between the following?

  ● a misunderstanding   ● a disagreement   ● a conflict

2 What conflicts have you experienced at work? How were they handled?

Listen to this   **3** 🎧 **48** Paulo Puente and Janine Elie are project managers in a company producing sportswear. Listen to them describing some experiences of conflict in international projects in their organisation. Complete this summary for each of them.

	Paulo	Janine
1 general reasons for conflict	lack of resources, poor planning	
2 example of specific conflict		A team member didn't follow the rules.
3 result of this conflict		

4 🎧 **49** What do you think is the best way to deal with the types of conflict mentioned in Exercise 3? Listen to the second part of the discussion and compare your answers to Paulo and Janine's.

5 Janine says, 'The best type of conflict management is actually about making sure conflict doesn't happen, avoiding it in the first place.' How far do you agree? Why?

Focus on language **6 a A good way of reducing conflict in meetings is to develop an open communication culture. Look at the suggestions (a–f) in the box below and match them to these phrases (1–6).**

1 Sorry, Pam, maybe there's something in this idea.
2 I think that's a good idea because ...
3 Luana, could you argue against that for a moment?
4 Paul, what do you see as the advantages of Sue's idea?
5 I'd like to hear what people really think about this.
6 If I can just pick up on what Gudrun said, maybe we could ...

Developing an open communication culture in meetings

a Motivate people to express their real opinions.
What's your honest opinion about this, Peter?

b Invite someone to respond positively to other people's ideas.
Lorenzo, what do you think of Marion's idea?

c Discourage people from disagreeing too quickly.
Jim, before you disagree, can we just think about this?

d Confirm and give positive feedback to another's ideas.
I think that's very interesting. I had a similar experience a few years ago.

e Suggest a creative proposal based on someone's ideas.
I agree with Alex and think we could even try to do more.

f Welcome alternative points of view.
Lucy, is there another way of looking at this?

---

b What other phrases could you use to communicate the above ideas?

Let's talk **7 Work in small groups. You are members of the core team of a large global project. You have received e-mails from members of the project located in different countries asking for support with project problems. Read the e-mails below and discuss solutions to the problems.**

a Before you discuss, nominate one of the group members to lead the discussion.
b During the discussion, everyone should try to use the techniques in Exercise 6 to encourage open communication.
c After the discussion, evaluate its effectiveness with these questions:
   ● Were participants motivated to work together and offer ideas?
   ● Were people encouraged and supported to give different points of view?
   ● Were ideas connected and the best ideas taken from each person to find a good solution?

To: Core team
From: Peter Hansen
Subject: Project support

Hi all
I am increasingly aware that some senior leaders in a number of our big departments here do not support our project. These leaders are regularly heard telling others that they don't think the project is worthwhile and that the money could be spent by the company in a better way. What can we do to deal with this situation?

To: Core team
From: Pedro Martínez
Subject: Project ethics

Hi
We are having some issues here with the new ethical guidelines on business gifts introduced from headquarters (not accepting any gifts greater than the value of €50 from business partners (customers, suppliers, etc.)).
Some of our project staff who are involved with external customers say it is causing serious problems. Customers in this culture like to give gifts, and refusing them is seen as impolite, particularly because the refusal is on the grounds that the gift is seen as a bribe.
Can you advise on ways in which we can handle this? Is there any flexibility we can exercise to show greater cultural sensitivity?

Think about it **1** How good at negotiating do you think you are? In pairs, exchange examples of a successful negotiation. Why was it a success in each case?

2 Experienced negotiators know how to structure a negotiation effectively. Look at these ideas and add some of your own. Compare your ideas to those on page 120.
- Agree the aims of the negotiation in advance.
- Be positive and optimistic about finding a solution.
- Begin by asking questions about the other person's aims and needs.

Listen to this **3** 🎧 **50** Jerry Graesborg is leading an IT project for a global automotive company, based in the US. He is calling Angela Schmidt to ask for some information. Listen and answer these questions.

a What does Jerry ask Angela for, and why?

b Why is it a problem for Angela to give the information asked for?

c What is happening on Friday afternoon which makes Jerry's request so urgent?

d What has happened in the project which has made it 'really challenging'?

e How does Jerry feel about Angela's behaviour?

f What does Jerry decide to do in order to deal with the problem?

4 How well do you think Jerry handled the conversation? Why? How would you have handled it differently?

Focus on language **5** Making proposals and counter-proposals (bargaining) is a key negotiating skill. Complete the proposals below made during a negotiation using the correct words from the box.

agree	authorise	guarantee	hit	provide	relocate	sign off

a If you do this, I'll .... a full training programme for you.

b I'll .... you with an independent budget for the project.

c If you like to work independently, we can .... that you just report once a quarter.

d I'll .... as much international travel as you need to be successful.

e What if I .... an additional month's salary as a bonus, assuming you manage to .... the project target on time and on budget?

f Would you be willing to .... to the headquarters?

6 Match each of the proposals in Exercise 5 with one of these counter-proposals.

1 *How about* two instead?

2 *If this* gives me an international qualification, you have a deal.

3 *What if* we said 'commute to' rather than 'relocate to'?

4 *Provided that* reporting is kept to twice per year, I would consider the position.

5 *Fine, assuming* the travel budget is committed for the full term of the project.

6 *That sounds great, as long as* we can agree the budget total.

7 a Use the phrases in italics in Exercise 6 to brainstorm five (or more) counter-proposals you could make, if you were the project leader in this negotiation.

Example: *What if you said you would pay for three flights home per year?*

b Role-play short conversations, with one of you as project leader making the counter-proposals, and the other as sponsor who responds.

Let's talk **8 You are going to take part in a negotiation concerning the involvement of Pierre Garnaid in an international project.**

Student A: See below.

Student B: Turn to page 96.

Read your role cards and prepare your strategy for the meeting by completing this table *before* you start:

negotiation points	preparation notes
My ideal outcome from the negotiation:	
The main arguments and influencing strategies which I will use:	
An acceptable fall-back position (a deal which I will accept):	

Student A

Klaus Birreg (project leader)

You are a senior Swiss IT manager located in the Zurich headquarters of a global insurance company. You are leading a high-profile international IT project (with a lot of pressure from senior management) to create a new European customer database – but you have big schedule problems!

- You need to increase Pierre Garnaid's participation in your project (he is from the sales department of the French business and supports the customer part of the project).
- Pierre currently devotes 25% of his time to the project (agreed with his French line manager, Jean Piaget), but you need to increase this to 100% over the next five weeks.
- You sent a very polite e-mail asking for more time, but you made it clear that you feel there is little scope for negotiation. You are facing severe pressure from top management – the topic was discussed in a global board meeting. You are annoyed that you got no reply to your e-mail.
- You know that it will not be easy to persuade Jean Piaget to let Pierre participate in the project full time. You have heard from colleagues that he can be very 'tricky' in his arguments. Pierre has also said that Jean believes this project to be a waste of time.
- Although Pierre is excellent technically, you feel that he is too fast at times. As a result, he often has to rework many of his tasks and so has fallen behind schedule. Therefore, it is only fair he should do more at this critical phase of the project to catch up.

You are now going to meet Jean Piaget to discuss how to increase Pierre's participation in your project. Prepare arguments to support your position during the negotiation. Think about an ideal outcome and also prepare a fallback position (a less-than-ideal outcome, but one which you are prepare to accept).

Afterwards, discuss the negotiation and how far you reached your ideal outcome. Discuss which of your arguments and influencing strategies were effective. Note down anything which you think you could improve next time you have a negotiation at work.

Think about it 1 **Discuss this question with a partner.**

In which work situations do you think e-mail can cause conflict?

2 **What do you think about this e-mail sent between two colleagues? Compare your thoughts with the analysis on page 120.**

Subject: Presentation mistakes

Julia
I just looked at the presentation you prepared for the customer meeting tomorrow. I found many mistakes with your marketing data, which we need to discuss. Please call me immediately.
Bob

Read this 3 **Read the article below, then answer these questions.**

a Why do some people prefer to use e-mail to resolve conflicts at work?

b Why can we 'get the message wrong' when we read e-mails?

c What is the 'worst-case scenario' referred to in paragraph 4?

d In which situations is it recommended that you ask someone to read your e-mails? Why?

e What advice is given regarding the copying of your e-mail replies to managers?

f What is the best reason for using e-mail in a conflict situation?

Dealing with conflict: Can't I just send an e-mail? ;-)

by David F. Swink

It is very tempting to use electronic media like e-mail, texting and messaging to deal with the inevitable conflicts at work. Conflict just doesn't feel good, and people generally avoid it. It may seem easier to deal with conflicts by e-mail, because you don't have to see the recipient's angry expression or hear their raised voice.

While the isolation from strong emotion may be a comfort to some, the problem with e-mail is that it cuts us off from the most valuable information in communication: non-verbal information like facial expressions, body posture, gestures and voice tone, all of which are vital to interpret the real emotions behind the message. The result is, we often get the message wrong.

Research now indicates that we use non-verbal information during communication even more than we thought, through our use of 'mirror neurons'. A Society for Neuroscience paper, adapted from Marco Iacoboni, describes mirror neurons as 'a special class of brain cells that let us understand the intentions and emotions behind actions'. When you see someone smile, for example, your mirror neurons for smiling also fire up, creating a sensation of the feeling associated with smiling. You don't have to think about

what the other person intends by smiling. You experience the meaning immediately and effortlessly.

However, our mirror neurons are not at work, and other communication cues are not present, when we are e-mailing; therefore, we miss a lot of information about what the other person is feeling and thinking. When we read an e-mail, we automatically try to figure out the 'tone', or the emotional undercurrent. We fill in the gaps with what we think the person is feeling or what their intention is. Most people fill in the gaps with the worst-case scenario, especially if they don't know much about the person.

Of course, we live in a virtual world, and e-mail must play a role in how we deal with conflicts. We just need to know how to use it wisely. Here are some tips for using e-mail when dealing with conflicts.

- Don't assume (negatively) why a person didn't respond to your e-mail or answered it in a certain manner. Intentions are invisible. Get more information.

- Monitor your emotions. If you feel angered by what you read, don't write an immediate reply and hit 'send'. You may regret it once you calm down, and then it's too late.

- Save a draft of your reply. Have someone review your draft, or read it yourself after you have cooled off, and then send it.
- Do not rely on emoticons :-) or text speak (btw) to convey emotions.
- Be careful with sarcasm and humor. Your message could easily be misinterpreted.
- Be careful with 'cc's' and the message they send. This may imply that you are telling on a person to their boss or colleagues.

Do not use e-mails in conflicts:
- when you've never met the other person face to face;
- when the emotional level is high;
- when the e-mail has gone back and forth with a person more than three times. This could mean that the issue is too complex to deal with by e-mail;
- if the e-mail fills the screen. Simply phone – the message is too complicated for e-mail.

Use e-mails in conflicts when:
- there needs to be a record of the interaction (the most common reason);
- dealing with conflicts where the emotional level is fairly low.

The best reason to use e-mail is in order to set up a first contact by phone or a face-to-face meeting, to properly deal with the conflict.

adapted from www.psychologytoday.com

4 Which tips and ideas in the article do you think are most important? Which do you disagree with? What other advice would you add?

Focus on language 5 The e-mail below is a revised version of the one in Exercise 2. It integrates many of the recommendations for effective e-mail writing from this section. Complete it with your own words, then compare your answers to those on page 120.

Subject: Customer presentation

Dear Julia
(a) .... are well and that your side of the project is going well.
Many **(b)** .... for sending me a copy of your presentation. I'm just
(c) .... to give feedback and to clarify a few questions, which I hope will
(d) .... us to fine tune the actual presentation.
Firstly, I **(e)** .... liked it. I think it gets the key messages across clearly,
from my point of view. I had a couple of **(f)** .... about the slides on
product specification. I **(g)** .... if these may be a little too detailed for the
customer. What do **(h)** ....?
I also thought, and this is just my personal **(i)** .... , that section 3 could do
with a few more up-to-date images. I have plenty of product shots on file if you
(j) .... help finding anything. I **(k)** .... that creating this
presentation is your responsibility in Communications, but the images we have
here may be useful to you.
If you think it is useful to discuss any of the above, please do not **(l)** .... to
come back to me. We can set up a phone call before tomorrow afternoon to talk
things through.
Very **(m)** .... of luck with the presentation!!
Best regards
Bob

---

6 What do you like/dislike about the e-mail in Exercise 5? What would you change? Why?

Let's write 7 Look at the two scenarios on page 92. Choose one and write an e-mail which begins to manage the situation effectively. When you have finished, exchange your e-mail with others. Give feedback on what works well and what *could* cause misunderstanding or potential conflict.

D Intercultural competence: Understanding team styles

1 a Around the world, many people are working in teams. However, in different cultures, people understand the word *team* very differently. Look at these pictures of leaders and teams, drawn by participants in an international management training seminar. What differences in attitudes to teams do you think they show? Compare your answers with the descriptions on page 120.

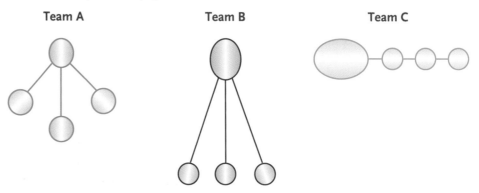

Team A   Team B   Team C

 b Which of the descriptions is closest to your own experience of teamwork?

2 🎧 51 Prachi Mishra is a project leader working in Mumbai for a Japanese retailer of electronic goods. She is heading an international team, which aims to improve the company's online sales. Listen to part of an internal presentation she is making to other project managers. As she describes experiences of teamwork in her project, note down what she says about:

- team roles
- leadership
- culture
- conflict.

3 a Prachi suggests that teams should set rules for team behaviour. She believes this can help to avoid conflict and also to deal with it, if it arises. In small groups, discuss and agree a set of the most important rules which you think can help international project teams to work effectively together.

Student A: Turn to page 93.
Student B: Turn to page 94.
Student C: Turn to page 97.
Student D: Turn to page 98.

 b When you have agreed your rules, present them to the other groups and compare your ideas.

Case study: Dealing with team conflict

Background José Losa Construction is an international building company. It is in the process of developing a global leadership programme. There are two main projects. The first is led by Andrew, who is from the US. Andrew's role is to find an international training provider. In his team is Kaneko, who is based in Japan.

Maria is leading the other project: to design and deliver a new learning management system for the company. Kaneko is a good friend of Maria's, as they spent two years working together in Tokyo for the company.

Situation Maria has seen Kaneko come under a lot of pressure while working with Andrew. She is worried that he will suffer from stress, so she decides to e-mail Andrew about the situation.

To: Andrew Maris
From: Maria de los Santos
Subject: Meeting with Kaneko

Dear Andrew
I'm just back from Tokyo, where I spoke at some length to Kaneko. I was quite worried, to be frank, about how much pressure he is under in your project. He's a real high–flier in the company, but I know he finds working on this project really demanding. I'm not sure that you quite appreciate the pressures he is under. Kaneko and I talked through everything that was on his mind. He is now confident that he can fulfil his tasks within your project deadlines. However, this is something you need to keep an eye on, in case pressures increase further. It would be a good idea for you to build a closer relationship with Kaneko, to avoid this problem coming up again.
Best wishes
Maria

Tasks **1 Discuss these questions.**

    a What do you think are the main issues here?

    b What do you think of Maria's decision to e-mail Andrew in this way?

    c What would you have done in Maria's position? Why? Compare your answers to the commentary on pages 120–121.

2 Read Andrew's reply on page 121. What do you think Maria should do next? Why?

3 Neither Maria's nor Andrew's e-mail follows the advice given in this unit for handling sensitive issues by e-mail. Using what you have learned, rewrite Maria's original message or Andrew's reply. Then compare your e-mail with another group. Ask for and give feedback on what is good and what could be improved.

4 In small groups, brainstorm some guidelines for reading and writing e-mails based on the learning points in this unit. Compare your ideas with others in the class and agree the best three ideas for reading and the best three ideas for writing e-mails.

Speak up, Smythe, I know you've got an opinion. I told you what it was in my e-mail this morning.

www.CartoonStock.com

FRY.

Read through the key words and phrases below from this unit. Add any other useful words and expressions which you feel are important for you to learn. Make sure you find the time to review the words and phrases regularly and to use them at work.

Conflict verb phrases
manage conflict
anticipate conflict
discuss potential conflict
deal with conflict
avoid conflict

Dealing with challenges
struggle to meet a deadline
commit to a deadline
step into a role
moan about
be under pressure
ask for support
complain
be under-resourced

a breakdown in trust
a lack of resources

Negotiating verb phrases
negotiate _with_ someone _about_ something
explain (an ideal / a fall-back) position
clarify a position
make/accept/reject a proposal
make a concession
find / fail to reach / reach an agreement

Bargaining phrases
If you do this, I'll ...
What if I/we ...?
Would you be willing to ...?
Assuming you can ..., then I'll ...
How about –_ing_?
Provided that ...
As long as ...

Writing tasks **Choose one of these situations. Try to include at least ten of the project words above in your e-mail.**

1 You have asked an international project team colleague to send you some financial information about their side of the project in Italy by the end of the week. You have just received an e-mail from your colleague explaining that they do not have enough resources to collect and format the data by the end of the week. Write an e-mail asking for the information again, making clear that you need to present the data at a senior-management team meeting.

2 An international project team colleague has sent you, in confidence, an e-mail which is complaining about the management of your project. They are saying that the goals of the project are not clear, the project leader is seldom available to take important decisions, and that the teleconferences used by the project team are inefficient. Write an e-mail which helps to support your team colleague and move the project forward.

F Project management tips and personal action plan

1 Take a few minutes to reflect on these project management tips. How far do you agree with each one? Which do you think is most important, and which ideas are most useful?

TIP 1

Balance strong organisation with flexible planning, particularly in the early project phases, until you are sure of the environment. International projects tend to be characterised by more uncertainty and complexity than domestic projects. This can make it difficult to schedule and organise your project work effectively.

Ideas for better project organisation:
- Plan short-term milestones rather than long-term ones.
- Meet regularly to review progress towards these milestones and to set further realistic short-term deadlines.

TIP 2

Become an excellent negotiator. Project managers need to negotiate many things with many stakeholders. It is difficult to negotiate without first understanding the other person's situation (we need to understand their local country operations, we need to know them as people).

Idea to become a better negotiator:
- Listening is the priority; asking questions is the skill. Remember, if the other party does not feel that you understand their position, they are unlikely to be open to influence by your point of view.

TIP 3

Use e-mail sensitively. It is easy to wrongly interpret the written word. Write carefully, and make sure your positive intentions for writing are clear. We also have to read e-mails much more carefully and not assume negative intention on the part of the writer. In fact, it may be better to assume positive intention and reply with this in mind.

Ideas to become a better e-mail writer and reader:
- Don't send e-mails straight after you have written them. Save them as a draft and re-read them later when you have cooled down; redraft if necessary.
- When receiving e-mails which make you angry, exercise self-control. Wait a few hours before replying.

Personal action plan **2 Take 15 minutes to review the unit. Note down at least three important points you have learned and that you want to apply to your own projects. Then commit to a schedule to implement your learning and think about how you can check if you have been successful, e.g. ask for feedback.**

	what I learned and want to apply in my projects	when/how I will apply this in my projects	how I will check if I have applied it
1			
2			
3			

7 Marketing the project

AIMS

A To understand the role of marketing in projects
B To practise promoting the benefits of a project
C To manage change effectively
D To encourage co-operation

A Discussion and listening

Think about it

1 What is *project marketing*? Read this short description, then answer the questions below.

> ### Project management success depends on effective marketing
>
> Marketing plays a key role in the success of a project. To be successful, project leaders need to sell their project; people need to hear about it, understand what it does and see how it can help them. Project marketing means, for example, creating a brand – a name and a slogan for the project. Project leaders also need to engage people in the project and get them working actively to support it. If project marketing fails, then important people in the organisation won't participate or get involved. This lack of support can often lead to project failure.

    a Which example of project marketing is mentioned?
    b Why is it so important for the success of projects?
    c What is the risk of not doing it?

2 The description in Exercise 1 mentions creating a name and a slogan for the project. In which other ways can leaders and teams market their projects?

Listen to this

3 🎧 52 Dennis Hemmings works in Istanbul for an international bank. Last year, he was responsible for the local part of a project to reduce the number of bank branches internationally. Listen to Dennis talking to a colleague about the role of marketing in this project and answer these questions.
    a What percentage of branches were closed globally?
    b How did people in Turkey react to the project?
    c What kind of project marketing was done?
    d How successful was this marketing in engaging people with the project? Why?

4 **a** Dennis said, 'We had to be much more creative in explaining the reasons for the reorganisation.' How could he have been more creative? What would you have done?

    b 🎧 53 Listen to Dennis and compare what you thought with what he actually did.

5 Choose the correct options in italic to complete this e-mail from Dennis to Michael, who was leading the marketing of the project.

Dear Michael

As agreed, I am planning to **(a)** *switch on / launch* the new project site on the intranet early next week. It will enable us to **(b)** *announce / post* the project to the whole company and start to **(c)** *build / advertise* understanding of what we are trying to **(d)** *reach / accomplish*. Overall, I think it **(e)** *represents / demonstrates* the project in a much more professional manner than the last site. I have put the interview with the CEO on the homepage to **(f)** *give / assure* it maximum visibility. Before I **(g)** *publish / show* the site, please take a look through it – see the **(h)** *connection / link* below – and let me know what you think.

www.futurebusinessmodel.com/demo

If you see any problems with the **(i)** *copy / script*, or if you want to **(j)** *reduce / amend* anything, please let me know. I can then **(k)** *update / upgrade* it over the weekend and ask our sponsor to finally **(l)** *confirm / approve* it before we go live. Some of the pages could do with **(m)** *livening / living* up a little – they're a bit dull in places. But there was very little time to **(n)** *script / prepare* it, so I think we can be relatively happy with what we've got.

Looking forward to your comments,

Dennis

6 Give the noun forms of these key verbs from the e-mail.

verb	noun
announce	announcement
advertise	
accomplish	
demonstrate	
publish	
amend	
confirm	
approve	

7 Your organisation is about to start a project to improve employee health and fitness. There are a number of planned initiatives, including:

- tokens which can be used at health-food shops
- subsidised gym subscriptions
- training in stress management and healthy living
- free health checks on company premises.

In the past, similar initiatives have failed. Employees didn't take up the various offers made by the company.

You work in the 'Communications' part of the project and have been asked to develop the following:

a a short slogan for the project

b recommendations for innovative and effective ways to market the project

c a checklist of items to be included on the project intranet site.

In groups, develop your ideas and prepare a short presentation with your recommendations. At the end, everyone should decide which group has the best ideas.

Think about it 1 It is important for people leading or working in projects to be able to sell the benefits to those affected and involved. Sales trainees learn how to make an 'elevator speech'. Read this description and answer the questions below.

An **elevator speech** or **pitch** is a short summary, used to quickly and simply define a product, service or idea and its value proposition. The name reflects the idea that it should be possible to deliver a convincing message in the time span of an elevator ride – from about 30 seconds to two minutes. A variety of people, including project managers, salespeople and policy-makers, commonly rehearse and use elevator pitches to get their point across quickly, often with a success story, a little anecdote which proves the project has a value. In fact, it's an essential skill for anyone in business because, sooner or later, we all have to convince someone of something.

a What kind of information do you think an elevator speech should contain?
b Have you ever given one? Tell your partner about the experience.

Listen to this 2 🎧 54 Françoise Simone works for a global insurance company. She is leading a project to create a new online service for customers, in which they can make and track their insurance claims. She is talking to Marlene Gabon, who is responsible for customer service. Marlene feels that customer contact is best handled by phone. Listen to their conversation and write Françoise's notes under these headings.

- **Overall aim of the project**
- **Why the project is needed**

- **Specific benefits the project will deliver**
- **Success story from the project so far**

3 How effectively do you think Françoise promotes her project? Why?

4 The verbs / verb phrases (a–i) below are all useful when describing benefits in the categories shown in bold. Complete each group of three with a verb or verb phrase from the box.

achieve	align	bring in	enhance	ensure that we
grow	minimise	plan to	slash	

    a objectives   aim to / need to / want to / ....

    b targets   reach / exceed / hit / ....

    c implementation   put in place / introduce / integrate / ....

    d results   enable us to / allow us to / guarantee / ....

    e benefits   optimise / improve / upgrade / ....

    f risks   prevent / avoid / eliminate / ....

    g processes   standardise / harmonise / streamline / ....

    h decreases   lower/ cut / reduce / ....

    i increases   raise / boost / multiply / ....

5 Use as many of the expressions from Exercise 4 as you can to describe the aims, benefits and impact of different projects which you have been involved with in your organisation.

6 When making an elevator speech, we can use linking words to build powerful arguments. Connect these ideas, focusing on the linking words in bold, to create messages that 'sell' a project which aims to increase organisational capability to innovate.

    a We've had some excellent early project successes,

    b Our ability to innovate faster will be enhanced by this project.

    c The project will deliver much better risk management.

    d There was resistance in the early phases of the project from some departments.

    e The new project will allow us to focus on customers,

    f There are clear benefits to the branch reorganisation,

    g As a company we are going to have serious cashflow problems,

    1 unless we implement this cost reduction plan immediately.

    2 Nevertheless, everybody is now fully on board.

    3 especially for those working in the areas of sales and marketing.

    4 In addition, we will also see cost efficiencies in some areas.

    5 despite quite serious resource problems.

    6 As a result, we will make fewer mistakes in future.

    7 rather than worrying too much about internal processes.

7 Which other linking words do you know which can be used to build up arguments for an elevator speech? Can you make some example sentences with these words similar to those in Exercise 6 above?

8 Think of a project you have been involved with and prepare a short elevator speech which answers some or all of these questions.

    ● What are the key project benefits for the organisation?

    ● Why is it relevant for the listener?

    ● Why will the project be successful?

    ● What has been achieved so far?

    ● When will it deliver its main results?

C Professional skills: Managing change

Think about it **1** Internal company projects are often designed to bring about some sort of change. However, many projects fail because employees resist change. Look at this list of reasons why this happens. Which do you think are most important? What other factors make people fight against change?

- Change brings a lot of extra work.
- People often think (or know) that the change is not a good idea.
- There is a risk of losing jobs.
- Psychologically, people don't like what they don't know.

2 What can project managers and teams do to overcome this resistance?

Read this **3** Read the article below on resistance to project change. Match these summaries (a–g) to the correct paragraphs (1–7).

a People feel their personal identity is under threat.

b People are overworked and overstressed.

c People think there is a hidden agenda.

d People have emotional ties to colleagues and the past.

e People feel that they are not competent to manage the change.

f People genuinely believe the proposed change is bad.

g People fear the unknown.

Projects and the tricky business of managing change

So what makes managing change so difficult for project managers? Here are a few pointers and some ways to overcome likely resistance.

1 Making a change is risky. It means doing something new with no real proof that it will work. And that can make people afraid. Idealistic arguments ("We need to be one company") or vague promises of future rewards ("We'll be more efficient") will not be convincing. The case for change must contain hard facts and figures, so people really *know* what change means and that it makes sense. Operationally, setting up pilot programs that model the change is vital. For most people, seeing is believing.

2 We often form bonds of loyalty to the people we work with. Loyalty helped our ancestors hunt antelope and defend against the aggressions of hostile tribes. If you ask people to do things in a new way, they may feel asked to betray former colleagues who supported the previous system, especially if it means that others lose their jobs. Change messages and actions must honour the contributions of those who brought past success to the organization.

3 Change necessitates the learning of new skills, and some people think they can't do it. In some cases, they will be correct, and these people are not right for the future organization. In most cases, people can develop the necessary skills, but moving them toward change requires you to be an effective motivator. Additionally, successful change campaigns include effective training programs and coaching support, which creates self-belief and a commitment to learn.

4 If an organization has been through a lot of upheaval, people simply resist further change because they are tired and overwhelmed. That's when you need to do two things: re-emphasize the risk scenario that forms the rationale for change; and be very generous with praise and sympathy for the effort people have to put in to support the project.

5 If you promote change, you may be suspected of wanting to increase your own power or of withholding "bad news," such as impending layoffs or redundancies. Build trust by being honest and showing a genuine interest in the greater good of the organization. And if your change project is going to reduce the workforce, be open about that and support an orderly process of retraining, to help people plan their lives.

6 Sometimes change affects a person's sense of who they are. When factory workers do less with their hands and more with the monitoring of automated instruments, they may lose their sense of being skilled workers. When resistance springs from these roots, it is very powerful. To minimize its force, leaders must demonstrate how change can support a person's sense of identity and also offer ways to grow.

7 The truth is, sometimes, that management's idea of change is all wrong. Sometimes people are not being afraid or foolish when they resist. They just see that management is wrong. So it's important not to ignore people's reservations or objections. Take time to listen to skeptics, because some percentage of what they say will prompt genuine improvements to the change idea (even if some of the criticism will be based more on fear and anger than substance).

4 Read the article again and answer these questions.

  a Why is it that arguments like 'We'll be more efficient' may fail to persuade people to support a project?

  b How can coaching help people to change?

  c How should managers convince people to trust what they say?

  d What does the example of the factory workers example tell us about resistance to change?

  e Why should project managers listen to those who challenge their project?

5 What do you agree/disagree with in the article? Which of the ideas for managing resistance to change do you think is the most important? Why?

Focus on language **6 Put these phrases in the correct order to describe negative reactions to a project designed to improve customer service.**

  a high levels of stress / have been received / in the team. / that the project / a number of complaints / is generating

  b people redundant. / the project / is using / that management / many people suspect / to make

  c will not deliver / I'm concerned that / to the organisation. / the project / tangible benefits

  d the project / the necessary budget. / very few people/ can be successful, / believe that / doesn't have / because it

  e it's far too complex. / resistance to / there's a lot of / from those / the new software / who believe

  f because implementation / the project / so slow / has received / has been / over the last six months. / a lot of criticism,

  g during the design phase / of the project. / very upset / users were / were not invited / at the very beginning / that they / to participate

7 Work in pairs to create short dialogues.

Student A: Start the conversation with one of the negative reactions from Exercise 6.

Student B: Answer the criticism with a positive argument, starting with one of these phrases (or a phrase of your own).

We're confident that ...	We're satisfied that ...
Rest assured that ...	I guarantee that ...
Believe me when I say that ...	Frankly speaking, ...
To be perfectly honest, ...	I appreciate what you're saying, but ...
We believe that ...	We're going to ...

Let's talk **8 a In small groups, discuss some of the important changes that will happen to your organisations in the future.**

  ● Who will feel most challenged by the change?

  ● What should be done to fully engage these people in the change process?

  ● Which single measure do you all agree is most important to manage change?

  b Present and compare your ideas to the other groups.

D Intercultural competence: Encouraging co-operation

1 Many cross-functional project teams experience serious 'cultural' problems when working together. In such situations, culture is not a matter of nationality, but more the attitudes and priorities related to different departments in a company, e.g. IT, sales and marketing, research and development, finance. Look at these descriptions of two departmental cultures (as seen from the outside). Which of the four departments mentioned above is being described in each case?

a This part of the company tends to be very individualistic. People are generally very positive. Their focus is on targets and profit. As individuals, they usually have a lot of confidence, but to others their attitude can sometimes come across as arrogant.

b These people can be good to work with in projects, because they have a lot of experience. They are often well organised. However, they sometimes forget that they are a support service. Sometimes they say no to solutions which our employees really need. They can seem rather inflexible at times.

2 What cultural differences do you see between different departments in your organisation? How can this affect co-operation in cross-functional project teams?

3 a 🎧 55 Jayne Wright and Dmitry Karev work in the New York sales department of a global pharmaceutical company. They are presenting their plans for the development of a new crop protection product. Their audience includes colleagues from Research and Development (Marie) and Production (Javier). Jayne and Dmitry want to convince the group to support the project. Listen to Jayne and answer these questions.

a What arguments does Jayne use to promote the project to the group?

b What is Marie's concern?

c Why is Javier cautious about giving support?

b How typical do you think these arguments are of the different departmental cultures? How well do you think Jayne handles the situation? What could she do to sell her project to the group more effectively and get their support?

4 a 🎧 56 Listen to another extract of the meeting as Dmitry talks to the group. Compare his approach to your ideas from Exercise 3.

b How successful do you think Dmitry is in convincing the group to accept the project?

5 Dmitry convinces other people to co-operate with him using a three-step approach:

1 Explicitly acknowledge the other person's point of view:
   I understand what you're saying ...
2 Make a proposal to move forward:
   My suggestion is for us to ...
3 Invite a response:
   How does that sound?

Look at some more objections to Jayne and Dmitry's project from different departments in the company. With a partner, take it in turns to respond constructively to these objections and propose a way forward.

a	IT	We will need to create a new customer database. We don't have time.
b	Finance	The business case for this project is not clear enough. I can't agree to it.
c	Sales	The margins on this new product are too low. It's not profitable enough.
d	Purchasing	The suppliers of the raw materials for this product are not reliable.
e	Legal	We will need a lot of time to apply for / receive approval for the patent.

7 Marketing the project

Case study: Effective co-operation

Background Rashid works for a plastics manufacturing company with headquarters in London. He is part of a global innovation project run by Eila Sandberg, who is based in Stockholm. The aim of the project is to reduce production costs worldwide. Rashid frequently flies from Dubai, where he lives, to London to meet the rest of the project team.

Situation Rashid and the rest of the team are finding the London meetings difficult to manage. They find themselves marginalised on many occasions. Their two British colleagues often dominate the meetings. They are often very direct in their criticism of ideas from other teams. This e-mail is typical.

> Dear Rashid
> Thanks for your recent e-mail with the suggestion to adapt machine capacities in China. We have already looked at this, and it's really not viable. We're working on another solution and talked to Eila about this yesterday.
> John

Rashid has found on a number of occasions that Eila, the project leader, usually supports the British team's proposals, which are then adopted in preference to the ideas of others. This has meant that the allocation of project resources has been changed, with over 80% now dedicated to the UK team to develop their proposals (it was originally planned to be 20%). However, many of the UK team's proposals have turned out to be unworkable. This ongoing failure of UK-based ideas is beginning to cause delays to the project.

For Rashid, his British colleagues are showing an aggressive and competitive self-marketing approach. At the end of a recent London meeting, he expressed his concerns very openly to Eila Sandberg and the whole team. The British team members reacted to this criticism by restating their full commitment to work as a global project team.

Next steps Eila Sandberg, who has been extremely busy managing a number of other projects, is surprised to learn of this level of discontent in the international team. She decides to organise a teleconference at the end of the week so that everybody can discuss this matter further.

Task **Discuss these questions.**
  a What do you think are the main issues here?
  b What do you think of Eila's decision to organise a conference call?
  c How would you handle this situation? What kind of messages would you communicate to Rashid, to the British team members and to the rest of the team?

Read through the key words and phrases below from this unit. Add any other useful words and expressions which you feel are important for you to learn. Make sure you find the time to review the words and phrases regularly and to use them at work.

Marketing

Verb phrases

market yourself (self-marketing)
publicise accomplishments
publish/post/update/amend pages
produce a first draft
have quick wins

announce the project
launch an intranet site
draft / liven up a document
celebrate success
be a project ambassador

Noun phrases

project newsletters
project brand
project slogan

Verbs for organisational change

reorganise
streamline
lay people off
restructure
have an outplacement programme

restructure
harmonise
make people redundant
retrain

Verbs for attitudes during change

be resistant to
have objections to
feel loyalty to colleagues

have reservations about
be sceptical about
be overwhelmed

The elevator speech

The project will:
● enable us to raise/lower ...
● allow us to boost/cut ...
● ensure that we can multiply/slash ...
● guarantee that we can grow/reduce ...

Discussing risk

We need to prevent ... from happening.
We need to avoid ...
We can eliminate this risk by ...
We have to minimise the risk of ...

Responding to criticism

We're confident that ...
Rest assured that ...
Believe me when I say that ...
To be perfectly honest, ...
We believe that ...

We're satisfied that ...
I guarantee that ...
Frankly speaking, ...
I appreciate what you're saying, but ...
We're going to ...

Writing tasks **Choose one of these situations. Try to include at least ten of the project words above in your e-mail.**

1 A colleague in another country has just sent you an e-mail asking how you are. Write a short e-mail in reply explaining that you have just started working on a project. Outline in a few words the scope, purpose and specific benefits of the project to the organisation. Explain to your colleague that you can give more information when you meet at a conference event next month.

2 You are leading a project and have sent an e-mail to an internal colleague in IT asking for two people with software development expertise to work in the project. The colleague has written back indicating that your project is not a priority and that, anyway, there are no free resources to allocate to it. Write a reply which aims to move the situation forward constructively.

F Project management tips and personal action plan

1 Take a few minutes to reflect on these project management tips. How far do you agree with each one? Which do you think is most important, and which ideas are most useful?

TIP 1

Beware that project marketing is usually overlooked, partly due to a lack of competence among team members. During the staffing phase, look for those with a marketing talent and give them a relevant role.

Idea to help effective project marketing:

● Plan a budget to allow you to buy in external expertise from consultants or resources from your internal communications department.

TIP 2

Be sensitive to the challenges of marketing internationally across cultures. Selling messages in a foreign language may be ineffective. Yet translation is costly and also requires close supervision.

Idea to help cross-border marketing:

● Pilot campaigns in local countries, because concepts, images and slogans may be effective in one culture but totally counterproductive for the project in another.

TIP 3

Remember that, as a project team member, you represent your project – you are an ambassador for the team. Make sure you can communicate the vision, purpose and benefits of the project persuasively to different international audiences.

Idea to help you to represent your project effectively:

● Be able to deliver fluently a two-minute elevator speech which gets across the main benefits of the project to the organisation.

Personal action plan   2 Take 15 minutes to review the unit. Note down at least three important points you have learned and that you want to apply to your own projects. Then commit to a schedule to implement your learning and think about how you can check if you have been successful, e.g. ask for feedback.

	what I learned and want to apply in my projects	when/how I will apply this in my projects	how I will check if I have applied it
1			
2			
3			

8 Finishing successfully

AIMS

A To learn lessons from completed projects
B To develop skills for presenting results
C To think creatively about change in the future
D To reflect on improving personal performance

A Discussion and listening

Think about it

1 What kind of things need to be done by the project team and leader to close a project successfully?

2 What can team members do to make sure that what they have learned on the project is remembered for use in future?

Listen to this

3 🎧 57–59 Listen to three members of a project team reflecting on their experiences, as the project comes to an end. They all work for an international fashion group, which decided to set up two retail stores in Russia. Complete the table as you listen.

	main success	main mistake	consequence of mistake
1	opened stores on time		
2		relied too much on video conferencing	
3			asking people to do training courses when they're busy

4 a What do you think could have been done differently to avoid these mistakes? What would have been the benefits?

b 🎧 60–62 Listen to the same three team members reflecting on how they could have done things differently. Compare their ideas to yours.

5 What mistakes have you seen in projects? What did you learn from these mistakes?

Focus on language 6 Complete the e-mail below using the words from the box.

blame	defect	error	failures	fault	issue
omitted	overlooked	underestimated	wrong		

Subject: Project review

Dear Jak

Please find attached a first draft of the closing report for the project. I've highlighted both the successes and the **(a)** .... quite openly. But I have taken great care not to apportion **(b)** .... explicitly. To highlight the main **(c)** .... , I think the budget overrun indicates that we **(d)** .... the cost of involving external consultants. That was partly an **(e)** .... on my part, and I accept responsibility for that. The estimated time was plainly **(f)** .... However, the technical **(g)** .... in the software – which also had a cost impact and was only discovered at a late stage – was really nobody's **(h)** .... You will see that in the report I have **(i)** .... all the training costs, because we agreed that these would go to the HR cost centre. So I have not **(j)** .... these.

Mareke

7 **When we review mistakes and think about alternative actions, we can use these three steps:**

1 Identify mistake: *We didn't have enough time for decision-making.*

2 Suggest alternative: *If we'd decided more carefully, we wouldn't have wasted so much money in the end.*

3 Conclusion: *I should have scheduled in more time.*

Look at these identified mistakes. Write down sentences similar to those above to describe the alternatives and conclusions.

a Our schedule was unrealistic. We missed a lot of deadlines by not planning more carefully.

b We didn't prioritise communication. We didn't assess the team's English skills and so we had real communication problems in meetings.

c The sponsor was difficult to contact. We couldn't involve him, which made marketing the project very difficult.

d The team members were busy on other projects and didn't prioritise mine. Without having enough time, it was impossible to deliver the right quality.

e Roles remained unclear for a long time at the start of the project. Without agreed responsibilities, a lot of key tasks just didn't get done.

Let's talk 8 **Many projects finish with a 'lessons learned' meeting. Team members discuss what didn't go so well during their project, to learn what to do better in future.**

a **Make some notes about a difficult project that you were involved in. Think about what could have been done to avoid problems and ensure a better result.**

what didn't go well	
what could have been done to avoid the problem	
learning point(s) from this experience	

b **In groups, share your experiences. Use these questions to help you.**

- What was the mistake or problem, and how serious was it?
- What could have been done differently?
- How would this have helped?
- What did you learn from this experience about working in projects?

Think about it 1 At the end of a project, the leader sometimes makes a final presentation of results to the sponsor. Look at these notes, made by a project leader planning the objectives for such a presentation. Which objectives do you think are the most important? Why?

> ● Confirm that project targets have been met
>
> ● Highlight special achievements (e.g. give praise to team members who performed well)
>
> ● Raise unresolved issues (e.g. budget overruns, some objectives not met)
>
> ● Recommend ways to solve the problems
>
> ● Thank the sponsor for support, etc.

2 **Can you add any more possible objectives?**

Listen to this 3 a 🎧 63 Listen to an extract from a project leader's presentation to his sponsors. He is reporting on the success of his project, which was created to outsource training. Answer these questions.

    a How successful was the project, according to the project leader?

    b Which main challenge is mentioned?

    c What caused the project to exceed its cost targets?

    d What is the major issue which has not been resolved?

    e What is the proposal from the project leader to solve the problem?

  b How satisfied do you think the sponsor will be with the suggested solution? What difficult questions might be asked?

4 a 🎧 64 Listen to the next part of the presentation. The project leader is asked four questions and answers each one. Note down the general topic of each question and the main details for each answer.

  b How effectively do you think the project leader handled the questions? Why?

Focus on language **5 a** Put the phrases in the correct order to create sentences which a project leader might use during an end-of-project presentation to a sponsor.

  a Confirming that targets have been met

  all the / have been achieved. / I am delighted / major targets / to confirm that / of the project

  b Highlighting special achievements

  to acknowledge / of all the team. / this opportunity / to take / the hard work / I would like

  c Identifying any unresolved issues

  to discuss. / only one or two / there are probably / I think that / remaining issues

  d Expressing strong belief that issues can be resolved

  that we can / issues quickly. / I am / outstanding / resolve any / very confident

  e Recommending solutions to unresolved problems

  of months. / the implementation / for a couple / would be / my recommendation / for me / to support

  f Thanking sponsor for support

  throughout this project. / to express / my appreciation / for the support / I would like / of the sponsor

b What other things could you say to express the above ideas? What other important things might you say during such a presentation?

6 a Match each of these techniques which a project leader can use to handle difficult questions (a–h) with a sentence exemplifying each technique (1–8).

  a Disagree.
  b Agree / Give positive feedback.
  c Avoid giving a direct answer.
  d Show understanding if a questioner shows emotion.
  e Postpone discussion of a topic to another time.
  f Refer back to a previous discussion to support an argument.
  g Clarify a question.
  h State commitment to make something happen.

  1 I appreciate the frustration; the catalogue will be ready soon.
  2 I'll do everything in my power to support that.
  3 Well, it's difficult to give an exact date, as there are many variables.
  4 I think that's a very good idea.
  5 Actually, I don't think that's the case.
  6 You'll remember the meetings we had about this.
  7 It's perhaps something we could look at later.
  8 What do you mean by 'help'?

b What other language could you use to handle questions using the above techniques? Which phrases might be useful for handling more challenging questions?

Let's talk **7** Think of a project you were involved in and use these ideas to prepare a short end-of-project presentation, as the project leader. Give your presentation and answer any questions afterwards.
  ● Project title/scope
  ● How far project targets were reached
  ● Special achievements to mention
  ● Remaining issues which need action
  ● Recommended ways to solve the problems
  ● Expression of thanks to sponsor / steering committee

C Professional skills: The future of project management

Think about it   **1 How do you think project management will change in the future? Which skills will become the most important for project managers? Why?**

Read this   **2 Read the article on page 83 about the future of project management and answer these questions.**

    a Why is project management capability so important to companies such as IBM and Hewlett-Packard?

    b What mistake did some salespeople make in the past, due to a lack of project management knowledge?

    c Why might the technical knowledge of stakeholders be a problem in complex projects?

    d What problems can the management of virtual teams present to project leaders?

    e What is a 'stakeholder agreement'? Who is responsible for achieving it?

    f Why is creativity an important ability for project managers of the future?

3 Which points in the article do you agree and disagree with? Why? What else do you see as important for the future of project management?

Focus on language   **4 Read the e-mail below, sent from a project leader to her team, explaining serious changes which have to be made to the project following a board decision. Complete it using the words from the box.**

halve	rationalise	reduce	reinvent
rethink	revamping	reverse	revised

Subject: Future planning for the project due to unexpected changes

Dear all

I regret to inform you that the board intends to **(a)** .... the project budget in line with new cost measures it is introducing across the company. It's unfortunate, but what we need to do now is to think creatively about how to go forward, as we still have to reach our targets. I see it as an opportunity for us to **(b)** .... the project, to think creatively about how we are doing things.

I think we could **(c)** .... the project scope. The original brief for us was to develop a suite of six products for ten countries. I think we should **(d)** .... this to just five countries.

I also think we can **(e)** .... the way we have organised the project. I suggest that we focus our efforts on China to begin with, and put all our efforts into developing products there. This would involve **(f)** .... project roles and responsibilities a little. I am attaching a **(g)** .... project structure for your attention.

The board will review the situation in six months, and it's possible it will **(h)** .... its decision. This is still not clear, and I will keep you informed. We can discuss this e-mail and the proposed measures in our regular conference call tomorrow morning.

Let's talk   **5 You work for a global car manufacturer. Two years ago, it set up a talent management programme to recruit and develop young people to become the organisation's project managers of the future. The programme has not been as successful as hoped.**

You are going to take part in a meeting with representatives from HR, project management and the talent group to think creatively about ways to change and improve the programme.

Read your role cards and prepare your strategy for the meeting.

Student A: Turn to page 93.

Student B: Turn to page 94.

Student C: Turn to page 99.

Student D: Turn to page 92.

How project management will change in the future

by Harold Kerzner, Ph.D. Sr. Executive Director for Project Management International Institute for Learning, Inc.

IBM has more than 300,000 employees, with more that 70 percent outside of the United States. This includes some 20,000 project managers. Hewlett-Packard has more than 8,000 project managers and 3,500 trained project management professionals.

The future is clear. Project management is going to change. It will move center stage and become seen by all organizations as a core competence, necessary for the very survival of their businesses.

Towards "engagement project management"

Project management capability is already critical in IT services, where companies like IBM and Hewlett-Packard sell their own internal capability in order to win complex outsourcing deals. They have to convince their clients that they have solid project management skills, which will guarantee they can deliver solutions for clients' business needs over time. This kind of "engagement project management" approach seeks long-term relationships with customers on the back of excellent project management skills. Interestingly, this has led to big changes for sales forces in IT companies, who used to make the mistake of signing great contracts without thinking through the concessions which they made and the problems of actual service delivery. Historically, project managers "inherited" service projects from sales with underfunded budgets and impossible schedules. Today, salespeople understand project management and sell the company's project services alongside products and services.

Embracing complexity

Project managers are experts in how to manage traditional projects. These have well-defined scope, a realistic budget and schedule and a relatively fixed target, and can be managed with analytical thinking supported by forms, templates, checklists, and guidelines for each phase.

In the future, project managers must become masters of far more complex projects. Some of the distinguishing characteristics of complex projects include:
- working with a large number of stakeholders and partners, many of whom may not understand the technology of the project;
- dealing with virtual teams located globally, where key decisions on the project may be influenced by local management politics, culture or even religious beliefs;
- long-term complex projects that begin with an ill-defined scope, undergo numerous scope changes, and where the end point is moving rather than stationary;
- working with partners and stakeholders who may have limited project management tools and antiquated processes that are incompatible with the project manager's tool kit.

Understanding the value of creativity

For project managers to be successful at managing complex projects with diverse stakeholder groups, the following will become best practice.
- Agreeing success criteria: At the start of the project, the project manager will meet with all stakeholders to come to a *stakeholder agreement* on what constitutes success on this project. Initially, many of the stakeholders can have their own definition of success, so the project manager must take responsibility and force an agreement with excellent negotiating skills.
- Defining the right key performance indicators (KPIs): The project manager will work with stakeholders to define how to measure success and which KPIs each stakeholder wishes to track. It is possible that each stakeholder will have different KPI requirements.
- Working to reliable KPI measurements: KPIs have to be measured and tracked on a common platform. This may be the hardest part to realize, as not all of the team members or strategic partners may have the capability to track all of the KPIs, perhaps because their IT systems are configured differently.
- Becoming creative: This will perhaps be the most critical competence of all. Having the flexibility and openness to find new ways to do things, as inevitable changes across the international organization potentially make your project planning obsolete.

Are project managers up to the job?

Project managers of the future can feel secure that their role will be very important in the future. However, they will need to embrace complexity and uncertainty by showing stronger people skills and far greater flexibility and more creativity than in the past, particularly in relation to unforeseen problem-solving. It's a real challenge, and one which perhaps not all of today's project managers will be able to meet.

D Intercultural competence: Learning and developing

Think about it   **1**   **Which competencies do you think are important for working on international projects? Discuss this list and add other ideas. Which two do you think are the most important?**

- flexibility
- good level of English
- focus on goals
- self-awareness
- influencing skills
- willingness to learn
- ability to listen
- tolerance of uncertainty

2   **How far do you think you have these competencies? Which are most important for you to develop? How easy is it for you to develop them?**

Listen to this   **3**   🎧 **65** **Listen to Bob Jenkins, a project leader, having an end-of-project meeting with Julia Mazur, one of his team, then answer these questions.**

   a   What does Bob think is the main purpose of the interview for Julia?
   b   What does Julia identify as her main strengths?
   c   Bob asks Julia to think in a 'new way' about her strengths. What is this way, and why is it important?
   d   Why did the team feel unhappy at times?

4   🎧 **66** **Listen to another extract from the meeting and answer these questions.**

   a   What personal development action is agreed?
   b   Which question does Bob ask which makes Julia hesitate?
   c   Why does Julia think the interview was useful?

Let's talk   **5**   **In pairs, role-play a personal development discussion and develop an action plan. First, ask your partner to tell you their main strengths. Then ask how these strengths could be seen by others as a weakness. Finally, agree the steps that could be taken in future to be more effective.**

personal development plan for future projects	
I see my main strengths as:	Others may see my main weaknesses as:
Personal development steps to become more effective:	

Case study: Celebrating success

Background Helena Lennerhov works for a major telecoms company. She has just finished a major international project. The objective was to set up a new payment service via mobile phones. Helena is delighted with the success of the project, which has finished on time and on budget.

Situation After members of the team had moved on to different projects, Helena decided to write to all the team members to express her appreciation.

> Dear everyone
> Just a short e-mail to express my appreciation for all your efforts during the project. We finished on time and on budget, which is a good result for the organisation.
> I hope we get the opportunity to work together again in the future.
> Good luck with your next projects!
> Helena

Helena receives this response the next day from David Drago, one of the project team.

> Dear Helena
> Many thanks for your e-mail yesterday. I appreciate the thought – many thanks. Just some quick feedback for you: I know that several team members were very angry with this e-mail. It created a lot of discussion yesterday afternoon, and I had a couple of calls from team members in the other countries. If you want to talk about this, I am in the office this afternoon.
> Best regards
> David

Helena is very surprised by this news from David. She can't understand how her e-mail could have exactly the opposite effect that she wanted.

Task **Discuss these questions.**
  a Why do you think Helena wrote the e-mail the way she did?
  b Why do you think that members of Helena's team reacted negatively to her e-mail?
  c How would you react to such an e-mail?
  d If you were Helena, how would you have handled this situation? What would you do next to improve the situation?

Read through the key words and phrases below from this unit. Add any other useful words and expressions which you feel are important for you to learn. Make sure you find the time to review the words and phrases regularly and to use them at work.

Project assessment
Nouns and noun phrases
a 'lessons learned' meeting
a failure
an error
a fault
an issue
a defect
a budget overrun
an outstanding problem
a project with a badly defined / ill-defined scope

Verbs and verb phrases

exceed (costs)	fail
underfund	underestimate
succeed	overlook
omit	blame
criticise	review the project

false/wrong/incorrect data
antiquated/obsolete/incompatible processes
unforeseen/unexpected problems

Change verbs

accelerate	broaden	grow	restructure	slash
adjust	cut	halve	revamp	slow down
alter	double	lengthen	reverse	stagger
alternate	drop	rationalise	revert	streamline
amend	enlarge	raise	shorten	treble

Feedback verbs
say thanks
express thanks/appreciation/gratitude
be grateful
appreciate
recognise

Writing tasks   **Choose one of these situations. Try to include at least ten of the project words above in your e-mail.**

1 You have just completed a project – it finished late and over budget. Your project sponsor has asked you to send her an e-mail with ideas on how similar projects could be run differently in the future. Write a short e-mail with three recommendations. Give reasons for your recommendations.

2 A tough international project has just finished. Write a short e-mail of thanks to a project colleague with whom you had close contact in your part of the project. Include some specific details of why you liked working with this person.

F Project management tips and personal action plan

1 **Take a few minutes to reflect on these project management tips. How far do you agree with each one? Which do you think is most important, and which ideas are most useful?**

TIP 1

Do a full review of a project after it has been formally closed. This involves in-depth interviews with major stakeholders, including the sponsor and steering committee, project-team members and the end users in the organisation.

Idea to help project reviews:

● Lessons learned should be captured in a structured document and made available to the rest of the international organisation to support wider learning and enable project management to become more efficient.

TIP 2

If you are a project leader, take time to run personal feedback sessions with each project-team member. Very often this doesn't happen, especially if team members are located in different countries. The objective of these end-of-project feedback sessions should be to identify areas of strength in personal style, as well as development points arising from less positive experiences of others who have worked with the individual.

Idea to help to run feedback sessions:

● Using coaching-type questions can be a good way to stimulate self-reflection in the person receiving the feedback so that they come up with the ideas on how to develop themselves.

TIP 3

Prepare thoroughly for the formal end-of-project presentation to the sponsor and steering committee. It may be useful to discuss the presentation with the sponsor beforehand to ensure that it is clear before the meeting what people see as the main messages.

Idea to help to run end-of-project presentations:

● Make sure you have answers prepared for any challenging questions which might arise concerning aspects of the project which were less than successful.

Personal action plan 2 **Take 15 minutes to review the unit. Note down at least three important points you have learned and that you want to apply to your own projects. Then commit to a schedule to implement your learning and think about how you can check if you have been successful, e.g. ask for feedback.**

	what I learned and want to apply in my projects	when/how I will apply this in my projects	how I will check if I have applied it
1			
2			
3			

Activity file

Unit 1, Section C, Exercise 5

Project tip

It is important in international project teams for everyone to properly understand the roles of other people in the team. This helps you to identify how you might be able to support others, or where others' work may have an important impact on your role. Learning about people's other work responsibilities is very important to understanding the possible pressures they may be under, and how this might impact on their productivity in your project.

Unit 1, Section D, Exercise 5

Case summaries

1 The takeover of the Baltic company by the Swedish company has created some resentment among Baltic staff, which has made co-operation difficult generally. The Baltic project team members come from a tradition in which leaders give clear instructions in a top-down way about what is to be done. The Swedish project leader believes that leaders should not tell team members what to do, but rather encourage them to make their own decisions and solve their own problems. This is why the Swedish leader seems to give unclear instructions for the Baltic team members.

   There are many ways to deal with this problem. As the leader, the Swedish manager could insist on using a coaching style. Alternatively, both parties could clarify their expectations of leadership and find a common way forward on goal-setting and decision-making which is clear and motivating for everyone. They should clarify when it is necessary to 'tell' and when 'asking' is acceptable.

2 The fact that a lot has to be done may have generated some of the frustration among the Australian team members. However, the real issue here is differences in communication style, arising from the different professional cultures of research-and-development scientists and marketing experts. This may possibly be made worse through differences in personality. The research scientists use a communication style which is typically fact-based, logical and analytical. The marketing colleague is used to a more creative and open style, possibly more extrovert, with ideas worked out during discussion rather than before the meeting. There is no single answer to this issue. One thing the research scientists could do is be more patient, listen more carefully and find value in what their marketing colleague is saying. Just insisting on rules, as they plan to, is really asking their colleague to conform to their way of thinking, which may demotivate and even offend him.

Unit 3, Section A, Exercise 9

Student A
Coach

You have been appointed to interview staff about how motivated they feel at the moment – in a particular project or in their regular job in the organisation. You are interviewing Student B. Ask them if they have any challenges. Coach them to come up with some solutions to any problem(s) or challenge(s) which they are facing.

Unit 2, Section B, Exercise 8

Student A

Situation
- You are part of a global project to standardise financial software across the organisation.
- You are from the North American part of your organisation, based in New York.
- You are at a project meeting in Paris and meet a colleague from the Madrid office.
- You know your colleague a little from previous meetings. Use the opportunity to have a social conversation, covering both professional and personal news.

Project news
The North American part of the project is going well. Everything is on schedule. Costs are a little higher than expected, due to the need to involve external consultants. Everyone in the organisation is excited about starting to use the new software. You have a very heavy workload at the moment.
You have been asked to participate in another global IT project, which will start in a week.

Personal news
It was your birthday yesterday. You plan to celebrate when you get home with a short trip to Chicago, your home town. You play guitar and plan to play with friends in a blues club when you are there.

Unit 2, Section C, Exercise 6

Commentary
E-mail 1
This gives some information, but is unclear in many important ways. The purpose for writing is not explicitly stated – is it to reflect on the user feedback or to propose a delay to the launch of the project?
The writer doesn't quantify clearly the extent of the negative feedback – only that there is 'quite a lot'. Also, the writer expresses disappointment, but not the reasons for that disappointment.
Finally, there is no clear outcome to the e-mail, only a thought that the user feedback could cause delays. There is no proposal for next steps or what action to take.

E-mail 2
This is clear at one level – the schedule overview has not been sent and should be sent in the afternoon. However, there is a risk that the reader feels criticised and the tone is blunt, if not rude. It is very likely to cause offence.

Unit 3, Section D, Case study

Chair
Your job is to facilitate a discussion of the different candidates and to help select the best one.
You would like to see David Bexley selected, so prepare arguments to help you in the meeting. However, you are open. If someone in the meeting has a candidate supported by stronger arguments, feel free to agree with their proposal.

Unit 3, Section C, Exercise 7

Project brief

The board of a major electronics retailer has voted to open an online store for the first time in its history. Historically, all sales had been made through its high-street stores. This move represents a huge IT challenge for the organisation. It is also a cultural challenge as, previously, store managers had been 'all powerful', able to set their own prices and to keep part of their store's profits. Now prices will be set centrally and profits will be posted to a central account. Efforts to introduce a similar development in the company failed three years ago due to lack of budget, poor planning and a great deal of internal resistance from many different sources.

Unit 4, Section A, Exercise 8

Student A
Project leader

Look at the schedule below, which shows the main milestones for your office construction project. Call your project sponsor to discuss the schedule. Exchange information, then agree an updated schedule, with new milestones and an end date.

Project notes
Task 1: Laying of foundations
- Completed by end February – two weeks ahead of schedule. Quality was 95% and on target.

Task 2: Building
- Bad weather is likely to delay building work to middle of April.

Task 3: Structural test with city engineers
- Due to delay with Task 2, you will need to agree a new date for structural test.

Task 4: Electrical installation
- This has already started, but technical problems mean there could be a one-week delay.

Task 5: Testing of electrical installation by city engineers
- Due to delay with Task 4, you will need to agree a new date for testing of electrical installation.

Task 6: Decoration of building
- Just started with first painting and office furniture installation (going well).

Task 7: Opening ceremony
- Will have to consider delay due to above technical and building problems.

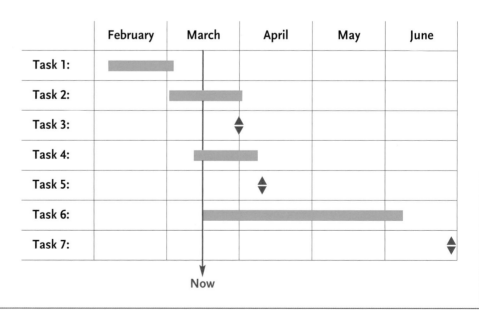

Unit 4, Section B, Exercise 5

Opening

Signal that it is time to start	*Let's **get** started.*
Welcome and apologise for any absences	*Apologies from Fiona. She's ...*
Confirm if agenda/documents received	*Do you all have a **copy** of the agenda?*
Introduce the agenda and objectives	*As you can see from the agenda, ...*

Handling the discussion

Ask for opinions	*What do you think about this, Jean?*
Give opinions	*My **view** is that we need to ...*
Clarify what was said	*Sorry, did you mean that ...?*
Prevent interruptions	*Please let Michel finish. Then I'll **come** to you.*
Focus the meeting on key points	*Can we come back to the **main** issue here?*

Closing

Move the meeting to a decision	*I think we need to make a decision.*
Summarise action points	*So, to **sum** up, we have decided to ...*
Check if any remaining questions	*Are there any questions?*
Promise to send minutes	*I'll get the minutes to you **by** the end of today.*
Confirm next meeting	*So, the next meeting is ...*
Thank and end	*Thanks everyone. Let's **finish** there.*

Unit 4, Section B, Exercise 6

If someone's communication style is causing real problems in meetings, it may be better to give some feedback in private rather than trying to manage things in the actual meetings. However, the following phrases may be useful:

Someone who is dominating
Can we get some views from some of the others?

Someone who says very little
Paul, would you like to comment on that? It would be good to hear your point of view.

Someone who uses complex arguments and is hard to follow
Can you simplify that a little for us?

Someone who talks about topics not on the agenda
Can we take that a little later? I'd like to come back to the agenda and look at ...

Someone who interrupts a lot
John, can you let Peter finish what he was saying? Then I'll come to you.

Unit 4, Section B, Exercise 7

Agenda

1 **Travel budget for projects**

The board has questioned the need for face-to-face meetings in international projects, as the company has invested in expensive audio- and video-conferencing equipment. It has asked that, in future, projects should be run more virtually, with no face-to-face kick-off meeting and only one physical meeting scheduled per year. Their argument is that unless a cost impact can be clearly demonstrated, this policy will be implemented. What is your response to this?

2 **Internet use**

A new study has just been published which indicates that private use of the Internet by employees at work is costing companies millions in lower productivity. Your board has asked you to produce a quick list of the pros and cons of introducing stricter rules to deal with this problem. You also have to come up with ideas for disciplining staff who break the new rules.

Unit 8, Section C, Exercise 5

Student D
Meeting participant (Human Resources Manager)
You are at the meeting today to suggest ways to improve the organisation's talent management programme for future project managers. Use the report below to prepare some creative ideas on how to make the programme more effective.

Management report – Current talent management programme

Target group: The current programme recruits 20 'young talents' per year in the 25–30 age range.

Advertising: The programme is only advertised on the organisation's website.

Selection: Based on one interview with an HR recruitment specialist

Training: A six-month internal programme, before assignment to a first project as a team member; completion of the six-month programme gives each young talent an internationally recognised qualification in project management.

Salary: In line with industry standards for graduate recruitment

Comments
Feedback from the programme has been extremely mixed.

1 *Feedback from talents*
   Training programme too long and boring. Want to start proper work asap. Salary level too low.

2 *Feedback from HR*
   Application rates for the programme are low; 70% of successful applications leave during first six months; 50% of the remainder leave three months after completing the training.

3 *Feedback from project managers*
   The selected talents are too academic and lack real work experience. Only 5% actually have the potential to become great project leaders.

Unit 6, Section C, Exercise 7

Scenarios

1 You have received what seems to be a very direct e-mail from a team colleague, informing you that a template for risk management which you sent was incorrectly completed (there was no quality data). Your colleague is demanding a new template with the correct quality data by the end of the day. They are not available by phone, because they are in a workshop. They can pick up e-mails if there is a problem. You remember discussing this issue at a meeting with the colleague last month. They told you that it was not necessary to send the quality data unless requested in advance. Accordingly, you did not send the quality data, as it had not been asked for. You are able to send the quality data, but it requires half an hour's work to extract it from the database.

2 You are furious. You have just left a meeting during which you and a colleague gave an update to the project team. You feel that your colleague made the project team believe that the excellent results were mainly due to his own efforts. The praise from the rest of the team seemed to be directed mainly towards your colleague. You feel this is very unfair and not a sound basis for a good working relationship.
   After the meeting, your colleague asked you to e-mail him your feedback on his part of the presentation. He wants to develop his communication skills. Generally, the presentation was very good, except for the matter which has made you very angry.

Unit 6, Section D, Exercise 3

Student A
- Working alone, read the five 'rules' below for team-member behaviour in international teams. Decide the most important rule on your list.
- In your group, take turns to read all the rules on your card out loud. Explain which rule you selected as the most important, and why.
- Ask the others in the group if they agree with your selection.
- Discuss and then, finally, agree as a group the most important rule on your card. You may have to change the selection!
- After you have discussed all the cards, agree as a group one more rule (*not* on any of the cards) which everyone thinks is important.

Team-member rules
- Make employee safety the number-one priority at work.
- Don't say negative things about others when they are not present.
- Don't listen to or allow others to say negative things about others when the person is not present.
- Be accountable for own actions, behaviour and choices.
- Don't complain about work situations – be positive at all times.

Unit 8, Section C, Exercise 5

Student A
Meeting leader
Use the report below to prepare some creative ideas on how to make the programme more effective.

Management report – Current talent management programme
Target group: The current programme recruits 20 'young talents' per year in the 25–30 age range.
Advertising: The programme is only advertised on the organisation's website.
Selection: Based on one interview with an HR recruitment specialist
Training: A six-month internal programme, before assignment to a first project as a team member; completion of the six-month programme gives each young talent an internationally recognised qualification in project management.
Salary: In line with industry standards for graduate recruitment

Comments
Feedback from the programme has been extremely mixed.
1 *Feedback from talents*
   Training programme too long and boring. Want to start proper work asap. Salary level too low.
2 *Feedback from HR*
   Application rates for the programme are low; 70% of successful applications leave during first six months; 50% of the remainder leave three months after completing the training.
3 *Feedback from project managers*
   The selected talents are too academic and lack real work experience. Only 5% actually have the potential to become great project leaders.

Unit 6, Section D, Exercise 3

Student B
- Working alone, read the five 'rules' below for team-member behaviour in international teams. Decide the most important rule on your list.
- In your group, take turns to read all the rules on your card out loud. Explain which rule you selected as the most important, and why.
- Ask the others in the group if they agree with your selection.
- Discuss and then, finally, agree as a group the most important rule on your card. You may have to change the selection!
- After you have discussed all the cards, agree as a group one more rule (*not* on any of the cards) which everyone thinks is important.

Team-member rules
- Don't try to blame things on others.
- Act professionally – know own job, do your own job, don't waste resources or time.
- Respect other people's opinions and invite their opinions.
- Listen sympathetically. Avoid being judgmental or defensive.
- Positively inspire other team members: encourage others, acknowledge their achievements and celebrate success.

Unit 3, Section D, Case study

Participant 1
You would like to see Lin Ho selected, so prepare arguments to help you in the meeting. However, you are open. If someone in the meeting has a candidate supported by stronger arguments, feel free to agree with their proposal.

Unit 8, Section C, Exercise 5

Student B
Meeting participant (young talent)
You are at the meeting today to suggest ways to improve the talent management programme. Use the report below to prepare some creative ideas on how to make the programme more effective.

Management report – Current talent management programme
Target group: The current programme recruits 20 'young talents' per year in the 25–30 age range.
Advertising: The programme is only advertised on the organisation's website.
Selection: Based on one interview with an HR recruitment specialist
Training: A six-month internal programme, before assignment to a first project as a team member; completion of the six-month programme gives each young talent an internationally recognised qualification in project management.
Salary: In line with industry standards for graduate recruitment

Comments
Feedback from the programme has been extremely mixed.
1 *Feedback from talents*
  Training programme too long and boring. Want to start proper work asap. Salary level too low.
2 *Feedback from HR*
  Application rates for the programme are low; 70% of successful applications leave during first six months; 50% of the remainder leave three months after completing the training.
3 *Feedback from project managers*
  The selected talents are too academic and lack real work experience. Only 5% actually have the potential to become great project leaders.

Student B
Project sponsor
Look at the schedule below, which shows the main milestones for your office construction project. Your project leader is going to call you to discuss the schedule. Exchange information, then agree an updated schedule with new milestones and an end date.

Project notes
Task 1: Laying of foundations
● You would like to hear that this phase is completed with 99% quality. If quality is lower, ask for an explanation why.
Task 2: Building
● Bad weather is likely to delay building work to middle of April.
Task 3: Structural test with city engineers
● You know that city engineers are only available to run structural tests on the 3rd and 25th of each month.
Task 4: Electrical installation
● You do not want to see a delay to this key phase of the project. If there are any possible delays, discuss the use of consultants to speed up the process.
Task 5: Testing of electrical installation by city engineers
● Organisation of electrical installation testing is the responsibility of the project leader – but you do not want to see any big delay, as this can impact on the opening date for the building.
Task 6: Decoration of building
● Check with the project leader that the colours used are in line with corporate brand.
Task 7: Opening ceremony
● You do not want to delay opening later than mid-July.

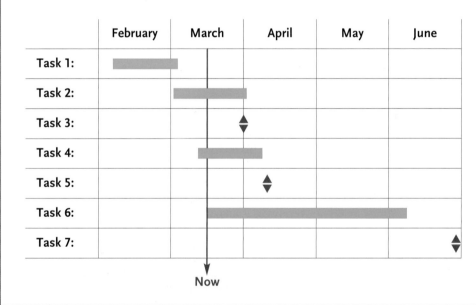

Unit 3, Section A, Exercise 9

Student B
Employee
Think about a problem or challenge which you are facing in your current project or normal job. Take this opportunity to describe it to the coach and develop some ideas on how to deal with the problem.

Unit 3, Section D, Case study

Participant 2
You would like to see Elio Ronzoni selected, so prepare arguments to help you in the meeting. However, you are open. If someone in the meeting has a candidate supported by stronger arguments, feel free to agree with their proposal.

Unit 5, Section B, Exercise 9

Participant
You are now going to participate in the teleconference to think of some recommendations to give to the Board.

a Take a few minutes to prepare two ideas to give in the meeting.
b You should also prepare some phrases to do the following during the meeting:
   ● interrupt someone (either to disagree/clarify, etc.)
   ● report a technical problem to the chair during the meeting.

Unit 6, Section B, Exercise 8

Student B
Jean Piaget (Pierre Garnaid's line manager)
You are a manager of the French sales department of a leading global insurance company. Pierre Garnaid, one of your best team members, has been involved in a new IT project led by a senior Swiss project manager, Klaus Birreg, located in the headquarters in Zurich. Pierre's task is to assist IT to develop a new European customer database which offers central benefits but few local advantages – in fact, the project seems to creates more complexity and work.
● The project leader has sent an e-mail saying that Pierre has to work full time on the project over the next five weeks. The e-mail was copied to a board member. You have not replied to the e-mail yet because of work pressure.
● Pierre has told you that Klaus has been extending the scope of his role *and* demanding too much focus on detail. As a result, the project has been occupying a lot of Pierre's time, even though he is meant to be participating only 25%.
● This project is causing problems for you in the French organisation. Pierre is not fulfilling his main duties there. There is an important customer event coming up in three weeks which will require a lot of effort from *all* members of your department to prepare. Pierre has skills which are essential for the success of this customer event.
● You have heard that Klaus is a poor time manager and often pushes for extra resources from country line management when his projects fall behind schedule. You do not want this to happen to you and so would not like Pierre to do more than the agreed 25%. You have heard that Klaus can be very defensive in meetings.
You are now going to meet Klaus Birreg. You would like to influence him to accept no further participation from Pierre. Prepare arguments to support your position during the negotiation. Think about an ideal outcome and also prepare a fallback position (a less-than-ideal outcome, but one which you are prepare to accept).

Unit 2, Section B, Exercise 8

Student B

Situation
- You are part of a global project to standardise financial software across the organisation.
- You are from the European part of your organisation, based in Madrid.
- You are at a project meeting in Paris and meet a colleague from the New York office.
- You know your colleague a little from previous meetings. Use the opportunity to have a social conversation, covering both professional and personal news.

Project news
The Madrid part of the project is not going well. There is a lot of resistance in many parts of the European organisation to the new finance software. Many people think the previous software is of higher quality. Delays to implementation are creating a lot of pressure for everyone.
You have a new job – to create a marketing plan aimed at convincing people to accept the new software.

Personal news
It's your first time in Paris. Your family will join you after the project meeting to spend a few days on holiday in the city. You plan to visit art galleries, as this is your big passion.

Unit 3, Section D, Case study

Participant 3
You would like to see Gisela Ebke selected, so prepare arguments to help you in the meeting. However, you are open. If someone in the meeting has a candidate supported by stronger arguments, feel free to agree with their proposal.

Unit 6, Section D, Exercise 3

Student C
- Working alone, read the five 'rules' below for team-member behaviour in international teams. Decide the most important rule on your list.
- In your group, take turns to read all the rules on your card out loud. Explain which rule you selected as the most important, and why.
- Ask the others in the group if they agree with your selection.
- Discuss and then, finally, agree as a group the most important rule on your card. You may have to change the selection!
- After you have discussed all the cards, agree as a group one more rule (*not* on any of the cards) which everyone thinks is important.

Team-member rules
- Focus on solutions rather than problems; always make suggestions.
- Be trustworthy – do what you say you will do, when you say you will do it and follow through.
- Treat everyone the same – do not treat some people as favourites.
- Be flexible – willing to compromise and allow other ways of doing things.
- Accept constructive criticism and learn from it.

Unit 6, Section D, Exercise 3

Student D
- Working alone, read the five 'rules' below for team-member behaviour in international teams. Decide the most important rule on your list.
- In your group, take turns to read all the rules on your card out loud. Explain which rule you selected as the most important, and why.
- Ask the others in the group if they agree with your selection.
- Discuss and then, finally, agree as a group the most important rule on your card. You may have to change the selection!
- After you have discussed all the cards, agree as a group one more rule (*not* on any of the cards) which everyone thinks is important.

Team-member rules
- Communicate effectively – speak positively and honestly, participate fully in meetings or discussions.
- Be committed to team success – share knowledge, offer help to others, support team decisions even if you sometimes disagree.
- Balance work and family life, know when enough is enough and it's time to go home!
- Don't take the job too seriously – it's OK to have fun at work.
- Accept that others may do things differently.

Unit 3, Section B, Exercise 9

Team member
You really want to take six weeks off from your project this summer to complete a personal goal (to do some voluntary work in South America). You discussed this with your project leader a week ago and got a very cool response. They are clearly not happy about the request, even when you offered to take it as partly unpaid.
You know that you are a highly valued employee. You feel that all your hard work and excellent results over the last two years in the project should create some flexibility on this issue from the company.

Unit 4, Section C, Exercise 1

- The goals are unclear.
- The budget is too small.
- There is resistance from the wider organisation.
- The team is spread over many locations.
- The sponsor does not have enough time to get involved in the project.
- The team members lack experience.
- The workload is too high.

Student C
Meeting participant (project manager)
You are at the meeting today to suggest ways to improve the organisation's talent management programme for future project managers. Use the report below to prepare some creative ideas on how to make the programme more effective.

Management report – Current talent management programme

Target group:	The current programme recruits 20 'young talents' per year in the 25–30 age range.
Advertising:	The programme is only advertised on the organisation's website.
Selection:	Based on one interview with an HR recruitment specialist
Training:	A six-month internal programme, before assignment to a first project as a team member; completion of the six-month programme gives each young talent an internationally recognised qualification in project management.
Salary:	In line with industry standards for graduate recruitment

Comments
Feedback from the programme has been extremely mixed.

1 *Feedback from talents*
   Training programme too long and boring. Want to start proper work asap. Salary level too low.

2 *Feedback from HR*
   Application rates for the programme are low; 70% of successful applications leave during first six months; 50% of the remainder leave three months after completing the training.

3 *Feedback from project managers*
   The selected talents are too academic and lack real work experience. Only 5% actually have the potential to become great project leaders.

Audio script

UNIT 1

Track 1

Interviewer: So, what kind of projects have you worked on together?

Bärbel: We've worked mainly on IT projects, where I'm leading from the headquarters in Europe and Alessandro is in Mexico.

Interviewer: What are the success factors in these projects?

Bärbel: Well, it depends a lot on the kind of project. But as a project leader, I generally look for technical skills: can the person do the job they have to do?

Alessandro: I think that here in Mexico, the main skill is social – you need to build relationships with people to get the job done. And more than that, you also need to be a good seller sometimes, too. You have to persuade people that what you're offering is really better than what they've got. I think for Bärbel, coming from headquarters, that's really important ... to have these selling skills.

Bärbel: For me, patience is also really important. Believe me, progress can be slow, things can get very complex, you have to change plans a lot.

Alessandro: No, no ...

Bärbel: Yes, it can be like that sometimes. And if you're not patient – and I'm not – you can get quite stressed. Then you stress others, and the project can often suffer with this.

Track 2

Interviewer: Can I ask you about your experience in these international projects? Is culture an issue?

Bärbel: Yes and no. I think for me personally, the biggest challenge is managing people from a distance. Most of the time, I'm in Europe and I have to work with people in different offices around the world. And distance makes it difficult to manage, to control what is going on.

Alessandro: Controlling is one thing, but the distance issue for me is more about trust. You need trust in a project, but building trust takes time and it needs face-to-face contact, so these international projects can suffer.

Interviewer: Interesting. But coming back to culture, Bärbel, I know you've worked in Mexico a lot. What's it like?

Bärbel: Well, I learned a lot. As an outsider, you really need to understand very different attitudes to time and planning. I still find it hard to adapt. I'm always pushing people to meet deadlines ... it can be frustrating.

Alessandro: Yes, but I think many people from headquarters spend too much time pushing. It causes frustration here, too.

Bärbel: Yes, it's funny now, looking back ... When you are dealing with big international projects, where there's a lot of complexity, sometimes if you work around structures and deadlines a little, doing it the 'Mexican' way if I can say that, it can work better sometimes. It means you don't waste time doing the wrong things, just following the plan. You become more creative and innovative and, actually, often end up finding better solutions than in the original plan.

Track 3

Jack: So, shall we get started? I would like to be informal, so feel free to interrupt and ask questions, because I know a lot of things are still unclear for many of you. I don't want to stand and talk at you for the next hour – I would like to have a discussion. I'd like to begin by reporting on my meeting with our sponsor last week ...

Track 4

Jack: It's nice to be able to start with some good news. I had a very good meeting with Petra – our sponsor – this morning and I can confirm that we do have her commitment for this project. So, to summarise and clarify, our objective is to create a single European learning and development organisation for the company, which will replace the local country organisations. The benefits include better-quality training at a lower cost, by pooling our resources. We need to work on a more detailed marketing message at some point. As for the project organisation, as you can see, we've divided the project into three parts: training courses, IT and managing our suppliers. The schedule is as planned, meaning we finish the project on the last day of December this year.

Track 5

Jack: So, any questions on that so far? Jon?

Jon: Er, yes, you didn't mention budgets at all.

Jack: I think this is going to be our main challenge – not enough money. We have a committed sponsor, but the budget is very tight for this – too tight, in my opinion. I'm trying to find other ways to solve the problem ... I'm working on various solutions.

Jon: OK. And, er, the deadline?

Jack: That's another problem. To finish according to this schedule is very challenging, so we need to go back to your line managers next week and discuss if we can increase your participation in the project, maybe by up to 20 per cent. I'll be setting up the meetings tomorrow, so just keep an eye on your mail boxes. OK, I'd like to—

Pam: Sorry, Jack, before you move on. Don't we need to review dependencies a little? We can't work in isolation on this.

Jack: Absolutely not, no. That's the final challenge, to map out and manage the various stages which are dependent on others. To deal with this, I'd like us to do some group work now, with you mapping out the main tasks and identifying where the dependencies are.

Interviewer: Why do you think this picture exercise is so useful in intercultural training?

George: If you remember, the instructions for the exercise were to 'describe' what you see. But it's interesting that when most people look at the picture, they normally write things like: *It's two boys fighting over a sweater* or maybe they say *They're brothers*. Some might be more creative and say, *Perhaps they're stretching the arms to make them longer so they fit better. In this way they're co-operating.*

Interviewer: Well, aren't these descriptions?

George: No, they're not descriptions at all – they're interpretations of the picture, they're assumptions about what is happening. This is the mistake that people usually make. Descriptions of the picture are very different and would be more like: *There are two young children. We can't be sure they are both boys. Both are wearing pants. One is wearing a T-shirt, the other has more of a vest-style top on*, and so on. A little bit boring, perhaps, but this is an accurate description.

Interviewer: But so what? Isn't it normal to interpret like this?

George: Yes, it is. We do it all the time. But when working across cultures, we have to be careful not to interpret and judge others' behaviour based on our own cultural values, because we can misinterpret things. Here's an example from real life: when I meet someone and maybe they don't smile or shake my hand, I might be very quick to interpret this as rudeness, because where I come from, this is a kind of impolite behaviour. But the person might not mean to be rude at all.

Interviewer: OK, but what's the solution? What's your tip for working across cultures?

George: Working with people from different cultures, we need to practise what I call 'creative thinking'. This means slowing down, observing and listening much more carefully to what people are actually saying and doing – this is the act of describing. And then we need to be much more open and creative in how we interpret things – try to think of how the other person is thinking, what values are driving their behaviour.

Interviewer: But is this useful in project management?

George: Absolutely. If project team members can practise this kind of creative thinking – listening carefully, checking interpretations, seeing the issue from different perspectives – then they can be better at solving problems. And being more open like this, I think also inspires trust and better co-operation.

UNIT 2

Interviewer: Can we talk a little more about planning? How important is project planning?

Meera: Running projects here in India, I think that good planning is really, really necessary. You need to have a clear project target, what you're trying to do, so you don't waste time doing the wrong thing.

Interviewer: And is this the same for both international or domestic projects?

Meera: Well, not absolutely the same. It depends on the type of project. Some need more planning than others. The thing to be aware of with international projects is that things can change during the project; goals can move if strategy changes; budgets can become a problem; key people leave, and so on. Last month, for example, I had to totally replan a big international project, because the sponsor changed, and the new guy decided to do things quite differently. So, my experience is that working internationally, you need to use what I would call 'flexible planning', both before and during the project.

Interviewer: But if things are more open, doesn't it make sense to plan even more, to manage the risks?

Meera: No. If you plan too much, it means you become less open, less flexible to what is happening in the organisation. Last year, I had the problem that another big project started after mine, and I had to share my staff, my resources with this project. That caused a lot of problems and delays for me. I know it all sounds a bit chaotic, but this is the reality in many organisations. And when people plan too much and try to stick rigidly to their plan in every situation, they get really stressed. They start to put pressure on other people to stick to the original plan and this generates conflict. And this makes it even more difficult to be successful.

Interviewer: I know you are in the middle of planning a kick-off meeting for a project starting next month. Tell me, how important is it to plan the kick-off meeting well?

Meera: It's very important. My main objective for next month's meeting is to make sure that people walk away with a very clear understanding of the purpose of the project – what has to be done and by when.

Interviewer: So should the main focus be clarifying the goal and tasks?

Meera: The task side is important, but for me, a second objective is to bring people together and start the process of relationship- and trust-building.

Interviewer: How will you do this?

Meera: In different ways. It's simple, but one thing is the round-table introduction – you know, when you say a few words about yourself – *I'm Marco from Italy, I'm in the design part of the project* – and so on. I think this is a very important opportunity to say to international colleagues who you are, what you do and why you are a good colleague to work with. So I e-mailed the people who are attending this meeting, asking them to prepare in advance for this – to make sure we get the most from this opportunity.

Interviewer: What kind of things will you say to introduce yourself?

Meera: Well, as leader, I'll be trying to inspire and interest people to work with me ... so I'll make sure I speak about my professional experience, my vision for the project, but then I will also try to spice it up in some way, try to say something unusual about myself – talk about a special hobby or a special experience ... something to show a little bit of myself.

Interviewer: And will you say anything about your leadership style?

Meera: Yes, I will talk about my working style – what

kind of leadership style works for me, maybe a bit about how I like to communicate, what kinds of e-mail I like, just being open and telling people about how to work with me ... so that we can create an effective team as quickly as possible.

Interviewer: Does this really help?

Meera: Yeah. I did this in my last project. It surprised a lot of people – they were saying to me after the kick-off, 'That was unusual, but really useful to hear.' In my last kick-off, I invited an intercultural expert to join us. He was there to build awareness of cultural differences in international teams. It was great fun and really got people talking about how best to work together.

Interviewer: A kind of intercultural team-building, then?

Meera: Yes, absolutely. And if I'm leading the project, I always make sure there's a team activity in the evening after the first day of the meeting – maybe the team cooks its dinner together ... whatever – but something easy and relaxed and fun. At the kick-off, it's all about getting relationships moving straight away.

Track 9

I'm a brand manager in Germany. I have a strong background in marketing. My main expertise is brand management, which might be useful in the project when it comes to communicating with senior management. In terms of my role in the project, my main responsibility is to make sure at the end of the day that we can sell the product successfully. And so the main outcome of my part of the project will be an advertising concept and campaign, which will convince customers to buy our product.

On a personal note, I'm originally from Regensburg. And when I'm not working, you'll probably find me in the ocean somewhere, as my big passion is scuba diving. Regarding working style, I can say that I'm very well organised. I like structure and planning. I always try very hard to meet my deadlines and I expect the same from others, too. I can be a bit reserved, quiet maybe, but I'm very interested in people. I like to support people, but it can take me a bit of time to open up. So please have patience with me.

And a final comment, I'd like to say that I'm very happy to be involved in the project, because I think the work will be interesting and is very important for the future of the organisation.

Track 10

Julia: Vadim, good to see you again! How are things in St Petersburg?

Vadim: Good. Busy as always. How about Hamburg?

Julia: Also very busy. So, are you still in training for the marathon?

Vadim: Yes, but I haven't done as much as I wanted.

Julia: When is it? Next month?

Vadim: Hmm, thanks for reminding me.

Julia: Ah, you will be fine. Anyway, how's your part of the project going?

Vadim: It's OK ... But things are taking longer than we expected. I'm worried about the end-of-the-month deadline. You know we have a big presentation to the board in St Petersburg.

Julia: What's the problem?

Vadim: Resources. We just don't have enough people to get all the work done. I need to speak to Geoff about it.

Julia: You need to, yes. We can talk later if you like. I think we're starting the meeting.

Vadim: Yes, let's talk later.

Track 11

Vadim: Vadim Abramov.

Julia: Vadim, it's Julia.

Vadim: Julia, nice to hear from you. How are you?

Julia: Good, how are you?

Vadim: Fine. Just out of one meeting and on my way to the next!

Julia: Well, I was just calling to see how your discussion with Geoff went. I missed you at the end of the meeting. I had to get my flight.

Vadim: It's nice of you to call. Geoff was sympathetic, but he couldn't really help. He has no more budget. I can't see how we will get all the presentations prepared. I told him – it's not just the actual presentations, we need to prepare sample materials, sample packaging ...

Julia: Look, can we help here in Hamburg? Joachim is a packaging specialist, you met him last month. He has some free time and said he can help.

Vadim: That would be really good. I'll talk to Ivan, who handles the packaging work here ... Can I get him to call you?

Julia: Fine. I'm in the office today and tomorrow. Afternoons are best for me.

Vadim: Fantastic. This is really appreciated, Julia. Thanks.

Julia: It's OK. So, I'll hear from Ivan later, then. Bye!

Vadim: Yeah. *Do svidaniya*!

Track 12

Mikhail: The main problem we had during this project was missing a lot of deadlines. Many international members of the team saw this as a big problem, but in Russia, we are more flexible with time. We can be late here, early there. The most important thing for us is doing the job well, meeting quality standards. And why else did we miss deadlines here? Nothing to do with culture; mainly because we didn't have enough people. The South Americans who set up the project didn't calculate the resources properly. But you know, this is a very 'can do' culture, so we don't complain. We just get on with it and do our best. And we usually get it right in the end!

Track 13

Jesús: The big problem has been getting people here to hit deadlines. There were a lot of complaints about resources, but I think it's really inefficiency. People don't organise their time well. It's a bit of a mess sometimes. But, you know, the people are great. They can produce real quality. It's no use just applying pressure on them. You need to be flexible. The main management tool is patience, partly, and also training, helping people get the skills to do the job faster.

UNIT 3

Track 14

Interviewer: OK, I'm here with Vladimir, Sophie and Kate. Vladimir, what have you found to be the main people-management challenge in leading international projects?

Vladimir: Well, because I'm very technical, I think it's very important to get people in the team with the right competence. In my last project, the people nominated to come in and join didn't really have the right technical skills, also English skills, to do the job properly. And that can make the project nearly impossible to manage.

Interviewer: But why were these people nominated?

Vladimir: There were different reasons. Firstly, they were available. Maybe they didn't speak good English, but they were the only ones in the department who spoke any English. We have this problem in our Moscow office. So I think one basic thing you need to do right at the start – I should have done this – is check that the people coming into your team can do the job – check the CVs of people applying for the project, talk to their local management about skills and so on.

Sophie: I definitely agree. It's been a big issue with me several times.

Interviewer: So, Sophie, other big issues?

Sophie: Kate and I were thinking about this, and for us the challenge is always keeping people motivated. Only yesterday, a team member was complaining about how much work she had – her usual job plus the project work on top of that. As a project manager, you need to recognise this and make sure that people stay positive and focused on their project tasks. If not, things just don't get done.

Kate: Yes, Sophie, motivation is the big issue, but you don't solve it with money. People need to understand clearly what they have to do ... you know, give them a clear role, give them support to do it and positive feedback when they've done it. It's really not that complicated, but I think too many project managers simply forget to do the basics.

Track 15

Interviewer: So is people management really just a question of team-building?

Vladimir: No, not really. I've noticed that we're focusing on internal team issues a lot here. But there is an external dimension, too – people outside the team. In most of my projects, the key person is the sponsor.

Sophie: Absolutely. You need the sponsor to push the project at key times, get you extra budget and resources and all that. But these people usually have a million other priorities, so getting them to focus on your project is difficult.

Interviewer: So how do you do it?

Vladimir: Well, I just have to keep knocking on his door, keeping him informed. And making sure I get a decision when I need one – like this week, I needed 250,000 euros of extra budget, and he was able to influence the board to get it. Simple!

Kate: And there's another group of key people in international projects: the local managers of the project team. I've had a lot of problems when local managers didn't support the international project. They often put pressure on their people to focus on local targets and not on the project work, and that created a lot of conflict. So I'm always trying to build relationships with these local managers, even though, technically, they're outside the project. It takes time, but it's an essential part of project leadership these days.

Track 16

Sabrina: So, José, how motivated do you and the team feel at the moment?

José: OK. It's a lot of work for everyone. But I think we are on track. We're still very motivated.

Sabrina: Very good. And how happy are you with my style of leadership? Maybe it's a little different. Am I asking people to do too much?

José: You give me and everyone else a lot of responsibility, which is great. That helps everyone, because they feel trusted.

Sabrina: But I sense there's some stress in the team. Is there anything about my style that demotivates you?

José: You know, the workload is very heavy. We had a customer event last week, which meant working 18 hours a day over two days. People would really appreciate more positive feedback when that happens.

Sabrina: What kind of feedback should I be giving?

José: Well, when you come here, you tend to focus on problems. Not much time is left for just saying, 'Good job, well done.' I know you think that, but you don't often say it to me or the team. And maybe telling our local managers here that good work is being done – that helps.

Sabrina: What do you think? Is feedback best given in the group or one to one?

José: Both.

Sabrina: OK, that's very useful feedback for me. I'll make sure I say something at the next team meeting about how well the project is going. And maybe I'll have a few more one-to-one meetings with people, including the local managers – just to give more personal positive feedback – as you said, to say 'Good job'.

Track 17

Madelyn: Hello, Madelyn Alvares speaking.

Haruki: Hi, Madelyn, Haruki here. Can I talk to you for a few minutes?

Madelyn: Sure. How can I help?

Haruki: It's about the design ideas. I've just had a look at the first samples from the consultants. I sent them to you last night. I'm a bit worried, to be honest.

Madelyn: I haven't had a chance to look at them yet. What's the problem?

Haruki: For me, the general appearance isn't serious enough. For one thing, there are too many colours. This is about health and safety, after all. And parts of the navigation are confusing. I think we need to go back to them for a new proposal, which means delaying the project.

Madelyn: But if we send it back to them, this is going to have an impact on the whole launch schedule. We have to meet the schedule.

Haruki : We can go ahead with this design, but the quality is not going to be right. I really think it's better for the project if we delay. If we roll out something sub-standard, the programme will be less effective. I know it's not good to delay, but ...

Madelyn: OK, I hear what you're saying. I agree with you we have to get this right, but I will need to discuss any decision to delay with the sponsor. He won't be happy. He's really committed to that deadline. I'll have a word with him and I'll call you later.

Track 18

Sam: Sam Jackson.

Madelyn: Hello, Sam. Madelyn here. How was Miami?

Sam: Wonderful! I could have spent a couple of months there. I got your e-mail about the e-learning design issue. Look, I'm really not keen on delay. You know that.

Madelyn: I know, but the first design quality is not good enough.

Sam: You're right, but this will have a cost impact. And we have the problem that HR and Learning and Development have other projects running with the same design consultants, so any delay here could have serious effects on these projects, too.

Madelyn: I understand. But it's a question of safety. If the e-learning effectiveness is reduced by poor design, we could have accidents. We need to have well-trained people. You know the legal costs if we get things wrong. Remember what happened in Brazil? I don't really see that we have any option.

Sam: But can't we ask the designers to respond quickly with a better design?

Madelyn: They have limited resources with all these other projects. I think we've put too much pressure on them, unfortunately.

Sam: OK. Look, go back to the designers and draw up a more realistic schedule. When we have that in front of us, we need to talk again about the actual delay. But it seems we have no choice.

Madelyn: OK, I'll talk to the designers tomorrow. I can get some idea of rescheduling to you after that.

Sam: Fine. Then we can talk again before the end of the week.

Madelyn: OK. Thanks, Sam. Bye.

Sam: Bye.

Track 19

Dialogue 1

A: Could you give a presentation next week to the management team?

B: I'm very busy.

A: I think it would be a great opportunity for you to be seen by senior management. It's very good personal marketing!

Track 20

Dialogue 2

A: I think we need to cut the training budget. What do you think?

B: I don't agree. If we cut budgets here, we're going to lose ground to competitors who do invest in training.

A: You may be right.

Track 21

Dialogue 3

A: What do you think we should do?

B: In my opinion, there is absolutely no alternative. We need to hire this guy. He's great.

A: OK, if you're sure ... Let's do it.

Track 22

Dialogue 4

A: I can't agree to this.

B: What's the biggest sticking point?

A: I think we have other priorities.

B: And what are they?

A: We need to finalise the end-of-year accounts. And we need to do forecasts for next year.

B: OK. Then maybe we can discuss starting the project after that?

Track 23

Dialogue 5

A: I really can't see the point of investing a lot of resources in surveying staff opinion like this. We know what people think. They're happy!

B: If it's resources that's the issue, I can lend you Bob to do this. He's very fast.

A: OK, that sounds good.

Track 24

Dialogue 6

A: Do we really need to invest money in intercultural training?

B: If you take a look at what our competitors are doing, it's becoming pretty much the norm in leadership training.

Track 25

Pavel: Ayla, I agree with most of this, but there are a few things which I don't understand. Why have you put me as 'high' and yourself as 'medium' in terms of project impact? You are leading the project – it's your responsibility. I think it's dangerous for a project leader to see their impact on a project as simply 'medium'.

Ayla: Yes, I understand. But my thinking here was, we're going to run into budget problems at some point. All projects do. And you're the only one who can actually get more money from the board. That's why I think you have more impact than I do.

Pavel: OK, I'm fine with my rating. But we need to upgrade yours. I don't think the board will accept a 'medium'. And I don't think it looks good for you.

Ayla: All right, we can change my impact to 'high'.

Pavel: Good. The only other thing I wasn't really happy with was the conflict-management training that's being proposed.

Ayla: For the team members?

Pavel: Yes.

Ayla: Why?

Pavel: I think it's too reactive. It means we expect conflict. We need to *avoid* conflict in the first place by having good proposals for the project, to get everyone's agreement and manage the change positively. Why don't we give people some change-management training, to get them ready to sell the change as well as deal with resistance?

Ayla: OK, I think that makes sense. It's taking a more strategic view of the situation.

Track 26

Michaela: As an insurance company, our culture is very much built around technical skills such as underwriting. It's a business where the products are not really that exciting – it's more about creating security and managing risks. And so you have what I would call a very analytical leadership, a lot of technical experts; you get to be a leader because you know the subject best. And this means the leadership style is a little top-down, more traditional, conservative perhaps. If you go into our staff restaurant, you'll see this in the way people dress. It's very formal.

Christiane: Interesting, it's very different here. Retail is much more dynamic. Leaders are more dynamic. Sometimes you have the feeling they're like cowboys in the Wild West – taking decisions quickly, independently. Here, you're paid to be an entrepreneurial leader.

Michaela: In our company, leaders spend a lot of time consulting their teams, to make sure that the right decision is going to happen. It's top-down, you know who the leader is, but there is a lot of consultation across the different levels. The main advantage of this careful style is that we usually take good decisions. But it is slow, which is a disadvantage when trying to innovate and bring new products to the market first.

Christiane: There are downsides to our leadership style, too. A lot of things are not co-ordinated and are implemented quickly – and mistakes happen. I just read on the intranet that we're stopping a huge project because it's overrun on budget by 25%. That's so typical. And you know, this expectation of rapid action creates a lot of pressure, with leaders demanding that things are done yesterday. But at the same time, if you're good, leaders will give you a lot of responsibility and freedom to take decisions, which can be very motivating for people.

UNIT 4

Track 27
Speaker 1
Satoki: Well, I'm from Tokyo, and the big problem here is staffing. It's a very dynamic environment. In Japan, people are very ambitious; they change jobs a lot, so you're always losing people from projects. They want to move to a better job and earn more money, and that creates a lot of problems.

Track 28
Speaker 2
Daniel: In my organisation, at least in the US part of it, the big problem is changing priorities within the company. I walked into my office last week for a meeting with my project leader, and he says, sorry, I've been asked to leave this project by a board member and take over another one, which is more strategic. And then the budget is frozen. All this just completely destroys our project planning. It's really frustrating!

Track 29
Speaker 3
Anna: I think the main issue for me is workload. In Germany, there's not enough time to get everything done in a working day, so people are always a little bit behind schedule. And you have to live with that, really. But you also have to manage it – which means sometimes you need to micro-manage; really pushing people to deliver each task, to get them to focus on your project and not on something else. But this kind of pushing, well, we don't like to do that. We prefer to trust people, show them the direction and then let them get on with the job. We don't like to manage every detail. So learning to do this is another challenge, but we have to do it to get results in these complex projects.

Track 30
Satoki: For me, quality is always more important than schedule. Delaying something but getting it right is for me better than just meeting a time deadline with 80% of the quality. So I am very happy. But I would expect this person to call me. I think it's dangerous to communicate about problems by e-mail, because you don't really know how serious these problems are without a discussion.

Track 31
Daniel: I don't like the e-mail. For one thing, he's informing his project leader too late. The deadline is next week and only now is he sending an e-mail. I always tell my team members to think ahead, to see problems coming and act before they even happen. And I don't like the fact that he's taking the decision to delay. For me, this is the project leader's decision to take. I think I need to have a long talk with this guy.

Track 32
Anna: Well, in one sense, I like the e-mail, because the person is actually telling me about the problem. I've worked in a lot of projects where people don't give you bad news until everything is about to explode. And I like the fact that the guy is confident that he can solve the problem and without any great impact on the project. So I don't have to do anything as project leader.

Track 33
Chair: OK, I think we'd better get started. So, firstly, let me say it's good to see everyone today. Welcome, everybody, except for Fiona. She had to travel to Chicago urgently, but I've spoken to her, so I'm able to give her opinions where necessary. In terms of agenda for today, which you all have ... good ... there are the usual items, some input from the sponsor, progress updates from each of you, a word from Klaus about quality; and then we need to discuss the communication issue as a separate topic. That's a question from the sponsor, but I'll say more about that in a moment.

Pedro: Aren't we going to talk about the budget today?

Chair: Um, not in detail. We don't have the time to look at everything today.

Pedro: But in Mexico, this is becoming a very big problem, and I think it will be for everyone.

Chair: Pedro, can we discuss this over lunch? I know it's important, so we should talk it through, but we have a full agenda with other issues.

Pedro: OK.

Chair: Good, then I'll begin with some feedback from the sponsor about the US side of the project ... and it's very good news in that ...

Track 34

Chair: So, the sponsor is asking us to rethink the use of consultants to support the marketing effort. It's a question of cost – they want to avoid hiring expensive people. What does everyone think?

Pedro: I don't really see the advantage of bringing in external consultants. I think we can do it ourselves. It's crazy to spend money we don't have on this, when there are other areas of the project which need more money.

Chair: OK. Katarina, your thoughts?

Katarina: Um ... I think that using consultants is a good idea—

Pedro: Yes, but it's important that we—

Chair: Pedro, let's hear Katarina, then I'll come back to you. Katarina? You were saying ...

Katarina: Yes, I think it's good to have some external input. It's an important project. We don't have the expertise in the team. If we do a bad job, the impact on the project will be significant.

Chair: Good point.

Paul: I don't agree. I think the money would be better spent on other things.

Chair: Paul, let's not dismiss things too quickly. What's Katarina saying? She said we don't have the expertise in the team. Is she right? I think she is. And she also said the impact of poor marketing could be significant. Paul, Pedro?

Paul: She's right.

Pedro: Yes.

Chair: OK, then let's think this through in a little more detail, because we really need to take the right decision.

Track 35

Presenter: Let me just turn briefly to the important issue of risk. I think as a team we need to work very hard in this project to tackle head on any major risks which could derail the project. What I want to pilot is some risk management, which will allow us to predict future problems and to put in place some effective contingency plans, which will mitigate the worst potential effects. The software also allows us to log risks in an Excel template, and then we can track things closely with a regular focus in our team meetings. We won't prevent risks from happening, but it means we are not exposed to potentially dangerous levels of risk. Of course, there will be cases where we simply have to tolerate risks – for cost reasons, perhaps. In such cases, I'm aiming to seek approval from the sponsor for any decision we make before we proceed.

Track 36

Michelle: The project has been very interesting. Basically, the task is to modernise a gas power station. And the main goal is very clear – to make it around 30% more efficient, which I think we can achieve. It's been a very tough project with very tight deadlines. And working with all these external consultants has been a real challenge. The consultants come here and work very intensively, perhaps 18 hours a day, for weeks and weeks. They are very focused, because they are working with bonuses – the sooner they finish the project, the bigger their bonus. But the people in the local organisation, they have to live here, they want to go home to their families in the evening. We're all professionals, of course, but we do have a life outside work. We had a big conflict here last week, when people had to work until ten at night to create a project report – people were very angry.

Track 37

Georgy: It's been a very difficult project for a number of reasons. The budget was a bit too low; some of the goals were unclear. I think the local project leadership was a little inexperienced in how to work with consultants like us. We fly in from all over the world for these projects. We are used to working very hard over short periods of time and delivering specific results. It's very important for local leadership to understand this and to explain to the local workforce how we need to work with them, to get things done. Here, it was not handled very well. It led to some conflict.

If I feel that the local leadership can't manage a project, I go directly to the sponsor, the CEO of the company, and get decisions there to help the project. I know it's not always good to do this, but it gets the job done faster. At the end of the day, it's all about getting results, isn't it?

UNIT 5

Track 38 (CD2 Track 1)

Roberto: One of the biggest problems I had was managing all those e-mails, especially during the pilot phase. It was ridiculous at times, maybe over 60 a day. I don't know if it was a language or a cultural thing, but the other team members never phoned, they only sent e-mails – and lots of them!

Nisha: Yeah, and the documentation was also a problem. One big headache I had was with all the PowerPoint files. In some cases, we had 20 versions of the same document – it was ridiculous! It was so confusing which one was the latest version. Do you remember the time I used an older version for that board presentation? It was almost a disaster!

Anne-Marie: Absolutely. I think what I remember most were the team meetings. They were so frustrating. The communication styles of the team were so different – some people very direct, some hardly saying anything, some just loved to talk – you know who I mean! And Pauline ... I think it was her first time leading a project, she couldn't handle it.

Roberto: That's right. But things improved a lot when Jim took over.

Anne-Marie: Yeah, he changed the communication on the project totally. We actually made a lot more progress once he came on board.

Roberto: Yeah, it was a bit formal, but his idea for e-mail rules, that really helped. No more than two e-mails per day to another team member, that was very good. And only copy people in if they absolutely needed to read the e-mail. That was probably the most important change for me.

Nisha: It was. And for me what was good, he gave me responsibility for keeping all the latest documents. Having one person in charge like that helped a lot, didn't it?

Anne-Marie: Yes, it was chaotic before. What I liked was that he spent a lot of time visiting all the locations. He came to France a lot, just to be there, to listen to how things were going, and that made communication work in the whole team much, much better.

Nisha: Yeah, and we did something interesting with meetings. What did he say all the time? 'Ask, not tell.'

Anne-Marie: That's right. He really believed in asking questions, listening, clarifying ... to get people to listen to each other rather than argue. To really understand each other.

Roberto: I still do all this. I clarify all the time now. 'What do you mean?' 'Why do you say that?' It really helps team communication.

Anne-Marie: What do you mean?

Roberto: OK, Very funny ...

Track 40 (CD2 Track 3)

Sam: So, Padma, we need a quick update from you on how the project is going in your region. What's the status of things?

Padma: Sure. Well, as you know, we're really under pressure with resources, so it's been quite difficult to make much progress in the last month. We're a little bit behind schedule on the product design ...

Marco: But that's really bad news! This is going to hold us up if we can't ...

Sam: Just a second, Marco. Padma, what do you mean 'behind schedule,' exactly?

Padma: Well, it's not too serious – one or two days. We're still confident we can hit the July deadline, as we promised.

Sam: OK, so no issues with the deadline.

Padma: Not really.

Sam: Why do you say 'Not really'? Yes or no?

Padma: What I mean is that, as of now, we'll hit the deadline, but if my boss suddenly drops a new job on my desk, I'll really be struggling.

Marco: But this is going to cause real problems. If—

Sam: Marco, she said 'if'. So, Padma, this means we can go ahead as planned, yes?

Padma: Yes. That's what I'm saying.

Sam: But we need to review things carefully, in case we need to give Padma more support if she comes under local pressure. OK?

Marco: Good. Sorry ...

Padma: Fine.

Track 41 (CD2 Track 4)

Electronic voice: *Petr is now entering the meeting room.*

Petr: Hello, Petr here.

Electronic voice: *Julia is now entering the meeting room. Kaito is now entering the meeting room.*

Petr: Good morning, Julia and Kaito. Petr here.

Julia: Morning.

Kaito: Hello, Petr. Hi, Julia.

Electronic voice: *Tomás is now entering the meeting room.*

Petr: Hello, Tomás. Welcome to the meeting.

Tomás: Thanks. Hello, everyone.

Julia: Hi, Tomás.

Kaito: Hello.

Petr: So, good to have everyone here on time. Can you hear me OK?

Julia / Kaito / Tomás: Yes, fine.

Petr: Good. So, how is everyone? Busy? Julia?

Julia: Very. Preparing for this meeting.

Petr: So, we're joined today by Kaito from Japan, who will be helping us to think about how we can roll out the project in Tokyo next year. Kaito, welcome, and maybe you can say a few words about yourself?

Kaito: Sure. I'm Kaito, ten years with the company, three years now in Tokyo, working with the CFO here mainly on strategy and planning. I can e-mail more of a profile, but for now ... I'm looking forward to working on the project!

Petr: Great. OK, then let's get started with the first item on the agenda. That's a quick update from Tomás on progress with his side of the project. Just to repeat our rules for Kaito for these calls: try to keep points short, try not to interrupt people. Oh, yes, Julia – as a native speaker, please remember the guidelines: speak slowly and clearly ... OK?

Julia: I'll try, I'll try ...

Petr: Good. Let's keep things interactive. If you agree or disagree with something, please say so, and if something is not clear. It makes my job so much easier.

Track 42 (CD2 Track 5)

Julia: ... so we may see a delay with Phase 1 of the project, because of these problems.

Petr: OK, thanks, Julia. Tomás, can I bring you in here for a moment? Tomás?

Tomás: Yes, sure.

Petr: What are your thoughts about this? You're likely to be the most affected by any delay.

Tomás: From my side, this is fine. In fact, having a little extra time is actually an advantage, to be honest.

Petr: Tomás, sorry, we lost you for a second. Did everyone get that?

All: No. / Not really.

Petr: Tomás, could you repeat that for everyone?

Tomás: Yes, I just said that it's no problem. It's good to have more time.

Petr: Good. Right, before we go on ... er, Julia, you have to drop out, I think?

Julia: Sorry, everyone. I have to attend a board briefing.

Petr: OK, no problem. I'll call you tomorrow morning to update you on the rest of the meeting.

Julia: Fine, OK. Bye, everyone.

Track 43 (CD2 Track 6)

Speaker 1

Where I work, people in meetings are very focused, they like to keep it short and simple. There can be plenty of silence, which gives people time to think. People don't like to be too direct. You don't hear much arguing in this organisation.

Track 44 (CD2 Track 7)

Speaker 2

This is a marketing consultancy with lots of creativity and emotion in meetings. We have some strong personalities here, too. Sometimes the only way to stop people is to interrupt them, and this is generally seen as fine. It's fast, creative and fun – and it works.

Track 45 (CD2 Track 8)

Speaker 3

Meetings can be quite intense here sometimes. The culture is a very technical one, with lots of information to exchange; so people may talk for a long time. You need to be a good listener to survive here – you have to listen to lots of information. Sometimes people can be pretty direct with each other, which I think surprises some of our international colleagues. It may seem rude to them. But it works for us.

Track 46 (CD2 Track 9)

Sarah: Sarah Miller speaking.

Patricia: Hi, Sarah, this is Patricia. I know you're very busy, but can we discuss Janek now?

Sarah: Yes, I got your e-mail. I'm a little surprised. Janek is very active in meetings with me. Maybe there is a relationship problem with you?

Patricia: Maybe, but I don't think so. His work is good. I try to give him positive feedback when I can. The problem is just in meetings. He's very quiet, and I need his contribution. It's becoming a problem.

Sarah: How good is his English?

Patricia: His e-mails are fine. But I've never heard him say much in English.

Sarah: Maybe that's the problem. In his job in Teltech, he didn't use English very much.

Patricia: OK, it could be that, then. I need to check this first before I do anything else. I'll have a talk to him, just to see how fluent he is.

Sarah: Good. Let me know if you have any more problems.

Patricia: Thanks, Sarah. Bye.

Track 47 (CD2 Track 10)

Patricia: Janek, I wanted to have a word with you about the team meetings. You say very little, and we need to hear from you. You have some very good ideas. Is it a language problem?

Janek: No, I can understand and speak English pretty well. Um, at the meetings, I think it's more my role to listen and support where possible.

Patricia: I agree we need your support. You know the Teltech environment very well. And we need to hear your ideas on how to manage that.

Janek: But I'm not a manager.

Patricia: No, I am leading the project, but you probably know better than me some of the decisions that we need to take.

Janek: But it's not my role to tell you which decisions to take. You are the leader.

Patricia: I know that. But your role here is to help lead this process.

Janek: I help if I can. If you ask me a question, I will give you an answer.

Patricia: But I don't want you to wait until I ask you something. It is your responsibility to give us your ideas and advice. I shouldn't need to ask you each time.

Janek: I'm on this project to support you and I will support you how I can.

Patricia: OK, Janek. I need to think about this. We don't see your role in the same way. Let me discuss this with your manager, and then we can talk again.

UNIT 6

Track 48 (CD2 Track 11)

Paulo: Most of the conflicts which I see are about resources – fighting over budgets or people, struggling to meet deadlines because of a lack of resources, a lack of enough people to do the work. We get this all the time, don't we?

Janine: Yes – so why does it keep happening?

Paulo: It's a good question! I think it's a problem of planning – or the lack of it, really. Many companies do this – they start projects, lots of them sometimes, but they don't plan them properly, and so project leaders and teams are expected to do 'mission impossible', reach very demanding targets when they don't have enough people, or the right people. And sooner or later you get conflict.

In my last international project, we had a conflict about poor language ability. Quite a few of the people in my team didn't speak good enough English. We had to get a lot of documents translated for them, and this really slowed things down and caused a lot of arguments. People in other parts of the company thought we weren't committed to the project, and that caused a big breakdown in trust.

Janine: But how can this happen?

Paulo: I think it's a problem of priorities in the organisation. You know, everyone's busy doing their own work, they have their own priorities and they don't have time to focus on your project – what you need from them at a particular time. It's really tough. What about you? Is it the same for you?

Janine: The biggest problem I find is about the differences between people. In international projects, people come together from many different areas; you have different nationalities, you often have different business functions and you even have external consultants, who often come from a very different organisational culture. And it's all these different approaches, the different viewpoints and working styles, that makes working together difficult. People often don't understand or tolerate the differences others have, and so it can become a negative experience.

Paulo: What sort of thing happens?

Janine: Well, three months ago, we had a huge conflict because someone in the Barcelona office had informally contracted an IT supplier to do some work on his part of the project. The project leader in Paris was really angry, because technically you need to go through the purchasing department to contract this sort of work. For the leader, it was a legal and disciplinary issue, and there was a huge row about it. In the end, the guy in Barcelona was asked to leave the project.

Paulo: I think there are a couple of things that project leaders can do about the resources problem. You need to be absolutely clear about what sort of budget is needed to achieve your target. And if the sponsor is not giving enough, you have to challenge the sponsor to get more funding. Tell them if they don't allocate the right budget, then the project's not going to be successful.

And the other thing is, when I'm recruiting a project team, I always make sure I get really motivated people, who are going to work 110%, who can give that bit more, to make sure things get done. That's often the most important thing.

Janine: In my last project, there was a meeting very early on, I think in the first month, to discuss the potential for conflict and what we could do to avoid it. That really got people thinking about how to work together. The other thing we did was to have very open and honest feedback discussions with each other every month. This was an opportunity to give positive feedback to other team members, but also to say what we didn't like and why. We could discuss issues together before they turned into problems. That's it, really – the best type of conflict management is making sure conflict does not happen, avoiding it in the first place.

Track 50 (CD2 Track 13)

Angela: Angela Schmidt.

Jerry: Hi, Angela, this is—

Angela: Yes, I got your e-mail asking for a report and a final launch date. The thing is, we're really very busy with user feedback at the moment. We don't have time to write reports. As I said at the last meeting, the priority now is to collect and analyse all the user feedback. This is taking a lot of time.

Jerry: But I need to send a report to the sponsor. I'm under a lot of pressure to get something to them by the end of this week.

Angela: I realise that, but we simply don't have the time or the people to write reports. And anyway, I can't give you a final launch date until we analyse the customer feedback.

Jerry: Angela, I need the report and a launch date. The sponsor isn't interested in excuses. He has to report on the project to the board on Friday afternoon.

Angela: But these are the facts!

Jerry: Look, this report has been in the schedule for around two months. You've had a lot of time to plan for it. And at this point in the project, you really should be able to give me an estimated launch date.

Angela: Jerry, we've had a really challenging time recently. I've had my two best people leave the project in the last four weeks. We're doing a very good job, despite getting no new resources. And I'm not committing my team to a launch date which is unrealistic. I'm sorry, but I can't deliver.

Jerry: That's very unhelpful.

Angela: I'm sorry, but that's the situation. You know we've been under-resourced. I've asked for your support on this many times. Sorry.

Jerry: OK. I need to think about this. I'm afraid it's really not acceptable. I need to talk to the sponsor again. I'll call you again tomorrow.

Track 51 (CD2 Track 14)

Prachi: I have to say that, overall, it's been a great experience so far working with this team. The project is a very innovative one. We've been working hard to be creative, to come up with new ideas on how to make the online customer experience better. And we have also come up with some very different ways of working.

The first, perhaps different, aspect of our team is in the team roles, which are not as strongly defined as in other projects – for us, they overlap. So one person may be working on design, another on navigation, but we really help each other at any time. We're there to give the other person ideas for their part of the project. For example, you'll see people just drop into the office of a colleague and say 'Have you tried so and so? Maybe this could help to solve your problem.' That's expected, and it helps to keep the atmosphere creative. And this also works for leadership. Yes, I have the leadership role formally, but I'm not standing above the team, I'm more in ... the middle of the team, I step into their roles, and they step into mine. I expect the team members to lead from time to time, to share leadership and be responsible for team success. It's not just up to me.

The only problem we have is with staff turnover – people leaving and coming into the project. You know, that's a problem with young, creative people – they get bored quickly, and we often find people leaving the team and moving on. So, to get any new team members quickly into our way of doing things, we have defined a set of team rules. We have said what is unacceptable – things like complaining about other people, being negative, not replying to e-mails, this sort of thing. And this has worked very well. We have been able to discuss how we should work together and we can avoid unnecessary misunderstandings and conflict.

UNIT 7

Track 52 (CD2 Track 15)

Colleague: Your last project sounded really challenging.

Dennis: It wasn't easy. The objective was to close down ten per cent of all local branches. You can imagine, this meant quite serious job losses. We had to ask people to move from smaller to bigger offices – that was a very difficult message to communicate.

Colleague: So marketing that project was really important?

Dennis: Yes, very. We needed marketing to create very clear, positive messages, because there was a lot of bad feeling about closing offices – plenty of people were saying 'I'm not helping this project.' If people didn't co-operate, it could mean the project taking a long time, and running over cost and schedule.

Colleague: So what did you do to market a positive message?

Dennis: Well, we did the usual things at first. We created a name for the project – 'Future business model' – being optimistic. We created pages on the intranet with basic information about the project – what we were doing and why.

Colleague: And did this work?

Dennis: Not really. We underestimated the communication challenge. People were losing their jobs, others were moving house. It was a radical change for a lot of people. We had to be much more creative in explaining the reasons for the reorganisation and the benefits of so much change. It was really very difficult.

Track 53 (CD2 Track 16)

Colleague: So what did you do?

Dennis: A couple of things. Firstly, there was a lot of suspicion that this was just a cost-cutting exercise, without respect for people. So we had to explain the business rationale, why it was essential for the company to reduce the size of the branch network. We asked head office to set up a web interview with the CEO, explaining what the company was doing and why. That helped a lot, because he's very highly respected.

Colleague: What else?

Dennis: We also worked hard to publicise what the company was doing for the people affected – helping them to find new jobs, offering retraining, support with moving home; and I think all this communicated the fact that the company cared about its people. This did make a big difference – people started to work with us and not against us.

Colleague: Did you do anything personally?

Dennis: Yes, I started having a lot more lunches with people ... It's important – spending time with people, hearing what they have to say and then explaining what we were doing and why. You know, sometimes listening to people is the best form of selling. If you give time to someone else, they'll take time to listen to you. I was able to convince quite a lot of people that way.

Track 54 (CD2 Track 17)

Françoise: Marlene, a couple of your people will be nominated as contacts for the new online service project. Can you recommend who they should be?

Marlene: To be honest, it's not a priority for me. You're planning to direct our customers to a website. For me, that's going to have a bad effect on the service we offer. Our customers expect a key account manager to talk to when they have a problem.

Françoise: OK, I see what you're saying. But with this project, we're aiming to actually improve customer service. It's good at the moment, but we want to make it even better. Research shows that we're behind the competition. Essentially, what we want to do is to enable you to do your job better, to focus on the really key customers.

Marlene: So how's it going to work, then?

Françoise: A lot of the customer service calls you handle now are really general enquiries – have you received my claim, how is it progressing, etc. All of that information we can put onto the website and let people track progress themselves. It makes things simpler for most of our customers. It increases service levels. It's

also much more convenient for them. For example, people can use it when they get home late in the evening. And our important customers, the company clients, not only get web access but also a key account manager. This person will be able to deliver a better, more personal service, because they will have more time. We've already trialled this in Italy, and the feedback has been 100% positive. It's been a real success story for us.

Marlene: So it's not all about cost cutting?

Françoise: No, not at all. Of course, we'll be able to get rid of unnecessary cost. But the main objective is to raise the quality of our customer service – letting you do your job more effectively where it matters, with key clients.

Marlene: OK. Maybe you could come to a meeting tomorrow with my management team? I think it would be good for them to hear this. There's been quite a bit of misunderstanding about this project.

Track 55 (CD2 Track 18)

Jayne: So, from our analysis of the customer surveys, there's clearly a demand for this product and a gap in the market. I'm convinced that we could sell it very successfully. What we need is support from you, so that we can put this proposal to the board for approval.

Marie: I'm concerned about the project schedules. They're much too short. You said that you wanted to launch at the end of next year. But surely we'll need a lot more time for testing? The legal framework has changed in recent years. It is much tougher now to get approval by the authorities. They want to see so much data, they take a long time to analyse it.

Javier: And there's a production issue, too. You're asking for new packaging for this product. That could be expensive to develop. I can't see an allowance for that in your budget here.

Jayne: There are some challenges with this, sure, but it's a great opportunity for us all.

Javier: It's a question of priorities. We have so many projects running, I have to be careful where I use our resources. And this one looks like it might require more time and money. For that reason. I'm cautious.

Jayne: I know we have a lot of projects under way. But this one is such a good opportunity!

Track 56 (CD2 Track 19)

Dmitry: Coming back to what you said about timing and legal issues, Marie: I understand what you're saying, because we had a few problems in this area last year. We underestimated the time it took to get approval for both of those products.

Marie: Exactly!

Dmitry: Jayne and I talked this through when we were developing the project plan. We took advice from the legal department. My suggestion is for us to have another meeting and go through this together in much more detail. How does that sound?

Marie: OK. I can see the appeal of the project, but this time we have to fully consider the implications of legal approval.

Dmitry: Sure. Javier, you're right that there will be costs associated with the new packaging and we can discuss that, too. In terms of priorities, we could look together at the projects you're involved in. Then we could see if there is room for what we think will be a strategic project.

Javier: Yes, that would be useful to do.

Dmitry: And if there is a conflict of priorities, well, we can discuss it at a more senior level. We can't decide this here.

Javier: OK, fine.

UNIT 8

Track 57 (CD2 Track 20)
Speaker 1

Well, I have mixed feelings about the project. In terms of success, yes, we opened the stores in both Moscow and St Petersburg on time. And as project leader, that was one of my main objectives. But now I have moved straight onto another project, for China this time. And there's no time to pass on what we learned in Russia to others, to the organisation. This is typical in big companies. They don't allow enough time to learn. It means that other people will make the same mistakes we did in Russia, and that will lead to more wasted money.

Track 58 (CD2 Track 21)
Speaker 2

I was responsible for the store design. I brought in experts from some of our other European operations to help. And it went well. We maintained the corporate brand, but we also integrated some design features which are very Russian. For example, we did a special photo shoot in Moscow. That gave us some great pictures of Russian models wearing our fashions. We put them on the store walls and that has worked well.

In terms of mistakes … in the early part of the project, we relied too much on video meetings with the retail-design consultants. It didn't work very well. If you want to collaborate, at least in a creative business like ours, you have to meet face to face, get to know each other and feel safe exchanging ideas.

Track 59 (CD2 Track 22)
Speaker 3

My role is to manage operations just after the project. Things are handed over to me. I will be in Russia now for the next 12 months. I have to make sure things really work. We have good sales, so operationally we are doing well. But things could be better. I think we made the mistake of thinking more about the stores than the customers. For example, no sales training was given to the staff in stores during the development of the project. It was all about building the stores. And my big problem now is asking people to do training courses when they are really busy.

Track 60 (CD2 Track 23)
Speaker 1

Looking back, what we should have done was to organise workshops immediately after the project, maybe with one of the external consultants, to capture what we had learned. We could have maybe posted a summary of this on the intranet. It would certainly have helped project leaders running similar projects in future.

Track 61 (CD2 Track 24)
Speaker 2

It's clear to me now that we should have created a travel budget to bring key people together in the early phases of the project. It would definitely have helped us to be more creative, and I think we would have made faster progress overall.

Track 62 (CD2 Track 25)
Speaker 3

I think we should have started recruitment and sales training right at the beginning of the project. So that when the stores opened, we had really qualified people welcoming our customers.

Track 63 (CD2 Track 26)

So, if we take a look at the next slide, this shows how successful the project has been. Training delivery has been outsourced, which was the main target. We have a very reliable, experienced provider in place, offering us a full programme of training services. And the service-level agreement is very tight, which will make sure the company gets the right quality. I have to say, it wasn't an easy project. Identifying the right supplier with the right quality levels was tough, but the whole team showed great commitment, and I'd like to say thank you to all of you today.

Now, to move to one or two other issues: finance first. You'll be aware that we had some resource issues during the project. We asked for more money to bring in two additional people, so there is a slight budget overrun. But this helped us to hit the deadlines successfully.

Probably the key unresolved issue concerns IT. We haven't had time to fully implement next year's online training catalogue, and this needs to be handed to someone in IT, I think, to complete. My recommendation is for me to be available to support IT with the catalogue. Any questions on this so far?

Track 64 (CD2 Track 27)

Questioner 1: Sorry, but I'm a little frustrated. I expected the catalogue to be ready by now. Many people in our department want to plan next year's training now, and this isn't going to be possible. I can't understand the delay. Why has this happened?

Presenter: I appreciate the frustration – the catalogue will be ready soon. I think we would have completed things, but, as you know, IT has been changing its systems, and in fact, they advised us to wait. But as I said, the catalogue will be available soon.

Questioner 1: When is 'soon', exactly?

Presenter: Well, it's difficult to give an exact date, as there are many variables … resources available, the status of IT … I would hope to see implementation by the middle of next month, or the end of next month at the latest.

Questioner 2: Can't the training provider help with this?

Presenter: What do you mean by 'help'?

Questioner 2: Well, perhaps they could create the catalogue?

Presenter: I think that's a very good idea. They have the expertise, but there will probably be some cost involved. Perhaps it's something we could look at later?

Questioner 1: But I still see this as the project's responsibility, your responsibility, really. My question is whether we shouldn't postpone closing the project. From my point of view, the targets haven't been met. Don't you agree?

Presenter: Actually, that's not the case. All the targets have been met. The catalogue implementation is outside the scope of the project. Our aim was to put in place an external training provider, which we have done. The catalogue issue came up during the project as an extra issue. We had a lot of meetings about this, if you remember, and we decided not to formally include this in the project scope, because it would mean increasing the budget. But we said we would do our best to implement it at the end of the project – which is what is happening.

Track 65 (CD2 Track 28)

Bob: So, Julia, what I'm doing with everyone in the team is taking some time to discuss how things went during the project. The main question is to see if there are some things you can do to improve your skills for the next project. Is that OK?

Julia: Yes.

Bob: OK. Well, I always like to start with strengths. So which strengths do you feel you have, which were helpful for the project?

Julia: Well, um, it was quite a complex project, um, I'm generally well organised – that's probably one of my main strengths – and I think that was very useful, especially at the start, when so much had to be planned.

Bob: OK.

Julia: I also always focus on quality. If something isn't good enough, I say so. I think that kept us on track in the middle of the project.

Bob: Yes, you had a lot of problems at that point.

Julia: Yes, people leaving the project, people with not enough time to complete their tasks. It was really important for me to manage that side of things, not just for my own work but for the others, too.

Bob: OK. But were there any times when those strengths of yours might be a problem for others in some way?

Julia: What do you mean?

Bob: Well, it's very important to understand how others might see us. So, your focus was on organisation and quality. Do you think that was always of benefit to the others?

Julia: I see ... Well, I know that some of the team sometimes found me – I don't know, maybe they would say 'inflexible'. I was always focusing on schedules and milestones and quality. Sometimes they felt there were other problems that needed to be sorted out first – like the resources, for example.

Track 66 (CD2 Track 29)

Bob: OK – so, what could you do differently next time?

Julia: Well, it's difficult. I still feel the highest priorities are schedules and quality.

Bob: OK ...

Julia: I suppose it's about communication. Perhaps I need to discuss more openly with the rest of the team why I'm pushing for certain things.

Bob: Mm. And maybe listen a bit more, too?

Julia: Yes, true. I am not the greatest listener.

Bob: So, these are good ideas. But how are you going to make sure you do them?

Julia: Well ... I think I need to plan meetings more carefully, with this discussion in mind. And probably I should also ask for feedback from colleagues ... am I doing enough for them? Is there anything else I could do to help them?

Bob: That sounds excellent.

Julia: Good. It's very useful to think about these things. Sometimes you need to be reminded!

Answer key

1 International project challenges

A 3 Bärbel: technical skills, patience
Alessandro: social skills, selling skills

4 a managing people from a distance, difficult to build trust
b different attitudes to time and planning
c People push others too much to reach deadlines, which leads to frustration locally.
d The 'Mexican way' is working around structures and deadlines. This is sometimes more effective because you can find better solutions.

6 a project overview **b** appoint **c** breakdown
d dependencies **e** risk assessment **f** stakeholders
g final testing **h** project review report
i lessons learned **j** success factors

7 *Suggested answers*
b do / run / carry out
c get / achieve
d get / give
e recruit / set up / manage
f define / agree
g allocate / assign / manage
h draw up / define / keep to / adhere to
i make / see
j run into / have / deal with / resolve
k deal with / solve / tackle
l complete / finish

B 2 He wants to be informal and is happy for people to interrupt him to clarify anything. He wants a dialogue with his audience.

3 a To create a single European learning and development organisation
b Better-quality training at lower cost
c training courses
d IT
e supplier management
f Complete the project at end of December this year

4 a Not enough budget, tough schedule and need to map and manage dependencies
b **budget**: Jack asks the team to be patient while he works on a solution.
schedule: increase the team members' participation in the project
dependencies: to be mapped out now in group work.

5 a **Using structure**
What I want to do now is to …
So, just to conclude …
As for project organisation, you can see …
b **Highlighting key information**
I'd like to say something important at the outset.
We need to realise that …
I'd like to highlight/emphasise/stress that …
c **Describing project organisation**
This part of the project is headed by …
The training team is responsible for …

d **Dealing with questions**
Does that answer the question?
OK. If there are no more questions, I'll finish there.
If you want me to clarify anything, just stop me.
So, you're asking if … . Is that right?

C 2 a Uninvolved sponsors or key customers playing political games; culture clashes that slow down project progress; resistance to the changes in organisations which projects often create
b Intelligent disobedience is knowing when and how to depart from the norm in opinions, cultural standards and processes.
c It means having the courage to scrap a project which may be important to you or another stakeholder, rather than continue with it until it inevitably fails.
d A 'fierce conversation' is an honest/truthful conversation which makes a situation clear in order to resolve it and move the project forward. The word *fierce* suggests that the conversation may stimulate emotion from others and so be challenging to handle or take part in.
e The risk is that you might upset a senior stakeholder or break an important rule or make a mistake – all of which could put your project and/or your own position in danger.

4 a managing **b** ensure **c** recruiting **d** designed
e drawn up **f** writing **g** runs **h** break down
i track **j** meeting

6 a structured **b** skills **c** motivated **d** commitment
e manage **f** deployment **g** people **h** orally
i focus **j** monitoring

D 2 a They interpret what they see rather than describe it.
b If we interpret the behaviour of others based on our own cultural values, we can easily misunderstand what is actually happening.
c He recommends slowing down and observing/listening more carefully. Also trying to understand how others are thinking.
d People can become better at problem-solving. It also inspires trust and better co-operation.

4 a **1** e, f **2** a, d **3** b **4** g **5** c

Case study commentary
The possible reason for the lack of information from Paresh to Jack is that Paresh's boss, the CEO in India, does not support the process of internationalisation represented by Jack's finance project. The CEO fears that it will reduce the independence and authority of the Indian organisation and give more power to the headquarters in New York. So the CEO has instructed Paresh to delay sending Jack the information until further notice.

Paresh understands Jack's request and wants to send him the information he has requested – he normally responds to such requests very quickly – but he cannot do so or tell Jack the real reason why.

Most people see this as a case revealing a communication or a cultural problem. In fact, it is neither, but rather a 'political' problem, which is often a key source of confusion and conflict in international organisations. Be careful not to decide too quickly that culture is the source of a problem.

Jack's decision to raise the problem with his own manager may or may not work. It may be that the only way to deal with the local CEO's resistance is to use the authority of higher management to force compliance. However, this process of escalation may risk turning the situation into a major conflict.

Building relationships and trust is important here for Jack. If he can build a closer relationship with Paresh, maybe then Paresh can tell him the real reason for the delay.

2 Getting it right from the start

A 1 *Suggested answers*

Many things need to be planned before a project starts, including:
- roles/responsibilities (who is doing what?)
- objectives/scope (what is the project trying to achieve?)
- organisation (how is the work to be structured?)
- resources (budget and human resources need to be defined)
- schedule (how long is the project / when is the final deadline?)

2 b *Suggested answers*

There are many different kinds of project kick-off meeting. The following are often integrated:
- speech by sponsor explaining the vision/purpose of the project
- overview of the project organisation and main tasks for each sub-project
- introduction of the project members
- clarification of actions
- discussion of risks to the project
- agreement on some principles of how to work together as a team
- team-building activity
- discussion of project schedule, agreement on short-term actions and setting of date for next meeting

3 a It's really, really necessary.
 b flexible planning, things are more open / the organisational environment can change
 c People get really stressed, they start to put pressure on people to stick to the plan and generate conflict / make project more difficult.

4 a a to make sure people have a clear understanding of the purpose of the project, and what is to be done by whom and when
 b bringing people together and starting the process of relationship/trust building
 c his vision for the project / professional skills / something unusual, e.g. a special hobby or experience
 d An intercultural expert was invited to build awareness of cultural differences in international teams. It got people talking about how best to work together.
 e a team activity, to help build relationships

5 a submitted **b** approved **c** proceed **d** appointed **e** assemble **f** co-ordinate **g** allocated **h** order **i** sort out **j** co-operate

7 a background **b** expertise **c** responsibility **d** outcome **e** note **f** originally **g** I'm not working **h** hard **i** have **j** involved

B 1 *Suggested answers*

project sponsor, business leaders affected by the project, external suppliers or consultants involved, etc.

2 Across cultures, the meaning of 'relationship' and the style of relationship building can differ enormously. In some cultures, people can be real friends at work, and socialise and mix with respective families out of work; in other cultures, work and personal life are clearly separated, and even in the office you are not expected to get 'too personal'.

3 a the marathon Vadim is preparing to run
 b She asks if everything is on track.
 c not enough people to prepare a presentation to the board
 d speak to Geoff

4 a to check the result of Vadim's conversation with Geoff about his project problem
 b She suggests involving Joachim, a packaging specialist, to help.
 c Ivan will call Julia to discuss how to use Joachim.

5 *Suggested answers*
- Begins positively.
- Asks about health: *How are things ...?*
- Asks question(s) with a social focus: *Are you still in training for the marathon?*
- Asks question(s) with a project focus: *How's your part of the project going?*
- Asks follow-up questions(s) to show interest: *What's the problem?*
- Asks question to offer support / give advice: *Can we help here in Hamburg?*
- Ends positively.

6 *Suggested answers*
 a up to **b** about you **c** imagine **d** difficult/problematic **e** problem **f** Great/Excellent **g** rest **h** How about / What about **i** same **j** Is there

C 1 *Suggested answer*

Increasingly, companies are working on projects with a global impact and so need to create global teams with members working primarily via electronic communication.

2 *Suggested answer*

Workers like flexibility and the ability to work from home / Best employees may be located anywhere in the world – diversity can be leveraged to the maximum. It may be more cost-effective to use staff from different parts of the world.

3 1 d 2 f 3 c 4 a 5 e 6 b

4 a to create time for people to get to know each other professionally and socially

b Provide team members with a single access point to necessary project information

c Because e-mail is an important channel of communication in virtual teams and it is easy to cause misunderstanding with poorly written e-mails.

d during video conferences or via e-mail with other team members copied in a distribution list

e The phrase indicates the problem that not seeing people on a regular basis as with co-present teams means it is easy to deprioritise project tasks in favour of other work. Project leaders need to maintain their own visibility and the connections between all team members with a mix of face-to-face meetings/visits, and regular telephone calls and e-mails.

5 *Suggested answer*

In some cultures, leaders are expected to lead and take primary responsibility for giving direction and taking decisions. In other cultures, the leadership is a shared responsibility between all the team members, with the leader co-ordinating decision-making and encouraging the team. In the latter model, team members are expected to show initiative and come up with lots of ideas as to how problems can be solved, to be available to support each other and not just fulfil their own role, and to do more perhaps than their formal job description.

8 b writing; express/say; support

c delighted; attend/make **d** regret; unable

e wish/like; happy **f** appreciate; let

g apologise; sooner **h** hesitate; further

i forward; meeting/seeing

D 1 *Suggested answer*

Feeling frustration in such a situation can be seen as natural. But it may indicate a lack of understanding of cultural differences on behalf of the American, or even a lack of tolerance for those with a different attitude to time. The Brazilian, on the other hand, could have apologised for the delay, in order to avoid any irritation at the meeting.

2 a missing deadlines

b culture (flexibility with time in Iceland and wanting to meet quality targets), not enough resources

c Doesn't complain and just gets on with the job.

3 His view is that deadlines are important, and time management can be a local weakness. But he appreciates the local commitment to quality, and thinks training can help address the problem.

Case study commentary

There is no single solution to this situation, as there are many possible explanations for what is happening. Both cultural and personality factors are probably involved.

Regarding Petra's situation, Birgit should acknowledge that Petra may be justified in her concern that Franco is missing deadlines and that she is right to want to impose a greater sense of discipline in the project. Petra's plan to discuss things with Franco is intended as a constructive effort at dialogue. However, it will be important for Petra to explore with Franco the challenges he faces with the project, in order to really understand what is going on. It could be that Franco has too much work and/or other priorities; he may lack competence to do the work as quickly as necessary; he may not understand the tasks he is given; or he may simply have a more relaxed attitude to deadlines.

Regarding Franco's situation, Birgit should ask Franco to clarify why the deadlines are unrealistic. She should also investigate the levels of demotivation, as this could be serious. She may also want to explain to Franco that he should talk to Petra and not to her. In terms of intercultural competence, Birgit will need to show influencing skills which can convince the two individuals to work together. She will need to show strong listening skills to understand the different points of view and some creativity in finding a solution which both find acceptable.

3 Managing people in projects

A 3

internal team challenges	solutions
1 Getting people with right competence **2** Keeping people positive about the project and focused on their tasks	**1** Check the CVs of people applying for the project, talk to local management about skills **2** Project leader should give clear role, support and feedback

4 a the project sponsor

b His sponsor influenced the board to approve extra funding for the project.

c Local managers of project team members. They can pressurise their people to focus on local needs rather than the needs of the international project.

d She builds relationships with them.

6 a **a** rewards **b** incentivise **c** acknowledging **d** driver **e** empowerment **f** praise **g** model **h** advance **i** conditions **j** benefit

7 a 4 **b** 6 **c** 5 **d** 2 **e** 3 **f** 1

8 a very motivated

b/c It's great to be given a lot of responsibility. It helps everyone to feel trusted.

d There's a lack of positive feedback directly and to own local management.

e Give positive feedback to the team.

f both

B 3 a To discuss his concern at the design proposals for the e-learning programme and to suggest that the project be delayed.

b The general appearance is not serious enough. / The navigation is confusing. / Design problems could make the programme less effective.

c He succeeds in persuading her to discuss the problem with the sponsor.

5 Arguments to persuade: Design quality not good enough

Sponsor objections: Increase in project costs; negative impact on other projects using the same designer

Deal with objections: No option; if people make

mistakes because not well trained, there could be accidents; reference to an incident in Brazil with high legal costs for the company.

Successful?: Yes, the sponsor accepts a delay, and re-negotiation of schedule with the designer will start the next day.

6 a 3 b 6 c 2 d 1 e 5 f 4
7 1 b 2 f 3 d 4 a 5 e 6 c
C 2 a 4 b 3 c 1 d 6 e 2 f 5
3 a They agree on most of the document.
   b rating of project-leader impact as medium (He thinks project leader is responsible and has high impact, so it's necessary to change the document for the board.)
   c They decide to raise the project leader's impact to 'high' and change the conflict-management training for team members to change-management training, as they think that it's better to avoid conflict in the first place want to help team members sell the project.
5 a 3 b 6 c 8 d 1 e 2 f 4 g 5 h 7
6 a overcome b engage c convince d tackle
   e commit f reassure g strengthen

D 2

	Insuro	Big Buy
key words	technical; analytical; top-down; traditional; conservative; formal	dynamic; take decisions quickly and independently; entrepreneurial
advantage	take good decisions	responsibility, freedom to take decisions
disadvantage	slow to bring new products to market	not co-ordinated; some mistakes made; lots of pressure

Case study commentary

People will make different choices according to their own criteria. All of the candidates have strengths and weaknesses. It is simply a question to decide which strengths and weaknesses are the most significant in this case. Additional measures to support the appointment, such as giving the leader a personal coach or some form of training, may be *very* important and should not be overlooked.

4 Keeping projects on track

A 3

speaker	problems
1	staffing changes / people leaving projects for other jobs
2	sudden changes in project priorities / staff reassigned / budgets frozen
3	heavy workload / change required in management style (micro-managing)

5 Satoki: Is happy to accept a delay if this ensures a quality outcome at the end. Would have preferred a telephone call.
Daniel: Doesn't like the e-mail because informing the project leader too late. Also thinks the decision to delay should be the project leader's.
Anna: Likes the e-mail because the writer is informing her about the problem. She likes the fact that the person is confident he can solve the problem on his own.
6 a on b yet c ahead of d In the meantime e by
   f shortly g As of today
7 a a postpone; amend b tighten up
   c reprioritise; ditch d swap e revisit
   f bring forward g replace h integrate
B 2 a thanks b say you will give her opinions
   c input from the sponsor d progress e quality
   f communication
3 a What does everyone think?
   b He insists that Katarina should be allowed to continue.
   c He asks everyone to stop and think about what Katarina said. They then agree she was right.
4 *Suggested answer*
The chair was effective in preventing Pedro's interruption and refocusing the group of what Katarina was saying. Generally, the style was quite assertive. Some will find this positive; others less so.
5 a get b copy c view/suggestion/opinion
   d come (back) e main f sum g by
   h finish/end/stop
6 Someone who argues
Challenge: 'Jackie, you seem to be against this. What's your proposal?'
Appeal to the arguer's team spirit: 'Helen, this is not a competition. Let's try to be as constructive as possible.'
Someone who is shy
Go to a breakout: 'OK, let's break out into smaller groups and discuss the problem. Jo, would you join my group?'
Prepare in advance: 'OK, let me summarise the views of everyone, which I collected in advance. Paul thinks ...'
Someone who complains
Reject blaming: 'Helga, I don't think we should blame others. That isn't fair if the other person is not here.'
Focus responsibility: 'I think we should all take responsibility for this situation and find a solution.'
Someone who talks a lot
Make clear there's a deadline: 'Mary, sorry to interrupt you, but we need to finish at four.'
C 1 *Suggested answers*
● unclear goals and objectives
● non-participative sponsors and stakeholders
● poor communication of objectives and targets across the team
● 'changing goal-posts': the project's scope or aims shift once it has begun
● lack of ways of measuring performance
● unclear responsibilities across the project
● poor resource planning

- poor supplier management
- lack of commitment or team-working
- lack of ownership

Source: www.pmis.co.uk

3 2 h 3 a 4 e 5 c 6 b 7 f 8 i 9 d 10 g

4 a a team members / experts outside the project with the right experience

  b People inside the project often see important risks, which can lead to project failure, but do not communicate this. The lesson is to have regular team communication about risk, e.g. make it a standard item on the agenda.

  c A showstopper is a major risk, which can lead to a project having serious problems or even failing. The answer is to prioritise the management of these risks.

  d When the effect on the project is minimal, or the chance to influence the risk is difficult, time-consuming or expensive.

  e A risk log keeps risks in mind and allows progress to be tracked. The document may also be useful to demonstrate that good practice was followed.

5 a a tackle **b** predict **c** put in place **d** mitigate **e** log **f** track **g** eliminate **h** exposed **i** tolerate **j** seek

6 *Suggested answers*

  a Let's look at steps we can take to get these people on board – for example, a series of meetings and 'get to know' sessions.

  b In that case, we should plan a few contingency measures. For example …

  c Can we run some early tests?

  d We should prioritise face-to-face meetings to build trust.

D 2 a to make the power station 30% more efficient

  b Intensive and goal-focused because they are driven by bonuses, which are higher the sooner the project is finished. Local employees don't work in this kind of way.

  c Local employees had to stay late one night to finish a report.

  d Leaders didn't explain to local employees how to work with external consultants.

  e He goes directly to the CEO/sponsor when necessary.

4 a original **b** direction **c** resistance **d** Willing **e** flexible **f** waste **g** local

Case study commentary

Csaba, as project leader, sees things primarily from his own perspective. He is concerned to keep his project on track. He is highly motivated to achieve his goals on time. Naturally, he is concerned to identify any risks to his project and to be proactive in dealing with them. Michaela's point of view is very different. As a global programme manager, she will be overloaded with work and have very little time available for all the people who need to speak to her. Many of her decisions will concern strategic matters, rather than the day-to-day operational issues which concern Csaba. She probably cancels meetings frequently not because she wants to, but because she has to.

Michaela is probably aware that everyone in the company is overloaded and that projects are not run in the best way. She needs and expects project managers such as Csaba to take more responsibility and act independently. She may feel irritated by Csaba constantly raising problems, rather than informing her of solutions.

Csaba's e-mail to Michaela is likely to be ineffective, as it is not discussing in any concrete way actual risks to the project. From her point of view, she sees only vague references in the e-mail and a request to take up precious time with another meeting. This is probably why she cancels.

However, as a senior programme leader, Michaela needs to understand and appreciate more the needs of her project leaders. She should have discussed her expectations of leadership more extensively with Csaba during the project kick-off meeting, so that he was clear about how she wanted him to operate. She may also need to show more flexibility in supporting him than she currently does. She is also prioritising her own needs above those of her staff.

In many organisations, project leaders adopt an approach to make transparent what needs to happen, why and when. So Csaba could write an e-mail which:

- explicitly states the actual risks and potential consequences of doing nothing
- proposes measures to deal with each risk, specifying the timing and any costs involved
- provides a timeline for Michaela to give feedback to the e-mail, after which Csaba will carry out his proposals (if nothing is heard to the contrary).

5 Building better communication

A 3 a managing a lot of e-mails

  b For language or cultural reasons, some people preferred to send e-mails rather than phone.

  c the large number of PowerPoint files and knowing which was the latest version

  d team meetings

  e differences in communication style / failure of project leader to handle the problem

4 E-mail: Established rules for using e-mail: no more than two e-mails per day to another team member; only copy people in if they absolutely needed to read the e-mail.

  Documentation: Having a single person in charge (Nisha), holding all the latest documents.

  Meetings communication: He spent a lot of time visiting all the locations, to listen. Encouraged the team to listen to each other rather than argue, to really understand by asking questions and clarifying what others were saying.

7 a a What's the status of things?

  b the meaning of *behind schedule* (said by Padma)

  c Why do you say 'Not really'? (She asks this because Padma sounds uncertain.)

  d So, Padma, this means we can go ahead as planned, yes?

8 *Suggested answers*

  a How much time?
  What do you mean by 'more time'?

So do you think you'll be able to finish the report by the end of the week?

b Which resource problems do you have?
What do you mean by 'resource problems'?
Will these problems have an impact on the project schedule?

c What are the main advantages?
When you say 'delay', do you mean to the overall deadline?
What are the consequences of such a delay?

d When do you think we should do this?
Interesting, why do you say we have no option?
Have you explored all other possibilities?

e How much data is unreliable?
Why is it unreliable?
How can we get more reliable data?

B 2 *Suggested answers*
Normal rules of effective meetings apply to teleconferences.
Planning: Conference calls tend to be more suited to less complex discussions with less variety of opinions. If complex issues are to be dealt with, a pre-meeting briefing of participants by the meeting leader may be useful.
During the meeting: Strong and clear facilitation is a real advantage. This means defining clearly the topic(s) of discussion, controlling who speaks (inviting and interrupting) and reformulating, to ensure everyone understands and has the opportunity to comment during and at the end of the meeting.
After the meeting: It is useful for the meeting leader to supply clear minutes and even to contact certain individuals by phone, to check levels of understanding and commitment following the meeting.

3 a He asks how everyone is / if they are busy.

b to briefly introduce herself, in order to familiarise the other participants with her background and role within the organisation

c She promises to e-mail a short profile. This avoids taking too much time away from the actual meeting.

d Try to keep points short; Try not to interrupt people (chair will do this if necessary); Speak slowly and clearly; People to say explicitly if they agree or disagree with something or if something is not clear.

4 a He may be the one most affected by any delay.

b He asks if everyone heard Tomás, then asks Tomás to repeat what he said.

c He promises to call her the next day, to update her on the rest of the meeting.

6 *Suggested answers*
Many of the ideas/phrases in the next column are also important in face-to-face meetings. But they are especially important in a teleconferences, where people cannot see each other.

chairing a conference call	example phrases
as people enter the call Check technology. Check local time/weather (small talk).	*Can everyone hear me OK?* *What time is it there?* *How's the weather?*
at the start of the discussion Confirm attendance. Confirm who is present	*Bob will be dialling in a little later, as he has another meeting at the moment.* *John, we have Claudia in Switzerland and Ben from the US already in the call.*
during the discussion Check understanding. Summarise what people say to keep things clear for everyone. Deal with people who have to leave the meeting early. Reaffirm the rules. Go around the group sometimes to check opinions.	*Did everyone understand what was said? Paul?* *Let me just summarise that, in case it was difficult to hear. Lars said that …* *So, Julia, I think you have to leave now, as it's three o'clock.* *Can I just remind people of the rule to …* *Can I have everyone's view on that, starting with Italy?* *Luca, what do you think?*
at the end of the call Ask for feedback. Ask for written agreement with the minutes. Give people a last chance to comment. Offer individual follow-up on specific issues.	*Can I ask for feedback from you on the call today? Lars, can we begin with you?* *Can I ask people to confirm their agreement with the minutes of the meeting by e-mail before Friday?* *Are there any (final) comments or questions before we close?* *Paul, I'll call you after the meeting to discuss the issue of recruitment, OK?*

7 a add **b** come **c** hand **d** stop **e** see **f** got **g** dial **h** make

8 *Suggested answers*
Could you move a little closer to the microphone?
Can you move away from the microphone a little?
You're very quiet/faint. Can you speak up?
You're breaking up a lot. Can you dial in again?

C 3 a Greater openness. It helps teams to learn and find ways to work more efficiently.

b It should begin by saying what people have done well.

c Never evaluate negatively or criticise someone's personality.

d The right questions encourage people to reflect on the consequences of their behaviour.

e People often react defensively. As a result, they are less open to learning and may be slower to improve their performance.

5 a Can I talk to you for a second?

b What do you think about this?

c Do you remember writing that?

d Can you see the impact it's having on the team?

e Is there another way to do things?

f When can you organise a meeting?

6 *Suggested answers*

1 Can we have a short meeting to discuss the event yesterday?

2 I'd like to give you some feedback on how you handled the event yesterday.

3 How did you feel it went?

4 I think your presentation was well organised and clearly stated the problems in the project.

5 You said at the beginning of the meeting, 'Senior management doesn't support this project.'

6 I think one or two of the senior managers were a little angry when they heard that.

7 What do you think about that?

8 How could you have handled it differently?

9 I think that sounds like a better way of handling things.

10 I think another thing you could do is to … What do you think?

11 So, just to summarise, how will you handle these events in the future?

12 How useful was this feedback for you?

D 2 1 plenty of silence for reflection, not very direct, little argument

2 creative, emotional, lively meetings, interruptions are common

3 intense, plenty of technical information, individuals talking for long time, direct style of address

3 a It can help us understand how we appear to others.

b Both are equally important.

c It encourages greater self-awareness when communicating.

Case study

1 a There are a number of possible reasons for Janek's lack of participation. One of the easy interpretations is to see it as a kind of resistance to the takeover. However, Janek comes from a research company and may have a scientific background. In this context, silent analytical thinking is the norm. It may also be a personality issue. He may be relatively introverted and feels uncomfortable speaking in front of others.

b The decision to discuss the matter with the line manager has some potentially positive outcomes: Sarah may be able to influence Janek to change his behaviour. But there is also the risk that Janek may feel that Patricia has 'gone behind his back' to his manager.

2 a a relationship problem with Patricia / not enough English language skills

b She decides to assess Janek's English during a conversation.

3 a Sarah could be right about the relationship with Patricia, in terms of her having the wrong interpretation of Janek's behaviour. She could also be right about his English skills, although this is less likely, as she probably knows Janek quite well.

b Patricia should have talked to Janek before now. It will be the best way of uncovering the truth.

4 a Janek expects Patricia to 'lead' by driving the project, taking decisions and checking with Janek when she needs to. Janek will only say something when asked to do so.

b Patricia says she is going to go back to Sarah to discuss how to resolve the situation.

5 **Case study commentary**

The problem here is a typical one in international teams – different expectations of the role of a team member and team leader. Janek expects Patricia to 'lead' and only occasionally check with him. Patricia expects Janek to be much more active in the decision-making process, as Janek has important knowledge about the Teltech organisation. Patricia's decision to go back to Sarah may improve the situation, if she is able to convince Janek to adapt his way of working. If not, it may create more pressure and potential for conflict in the project.

6 Dealing with conflict

A 1 *Suggested answers*

Many use the three terms as synonyms in everyday conversation. What distinguishes conflict from misunderstanding and disagreement is the intensity/seriousness of the difference of opinion and the level of emotion involved.

Misunderstanding

● a failure to understand; mistaking a meaning or intention

● a quarrel or disagreement arising from different interpretations

Disagreement

● a refusal to agree or comply

● a difference of opinion

● a quarrel or dispute

Conflict

● a sharp disagreement or opposition of interests, ideas, etc.

● an emotional disturbance resulting from a clash of opposing views

3

	Paulo	Janine
1 general reasons for conflict	lack of resources, poor planning	differences between people, lack of understanding
2 example of specific conflict	Not enough people spoke good English.	A team member didn't follow the rules.
3 result of this conflict	delays and breakdown in trust	Team member was asked to leave the project.

4 Paulo

● You need to be clear what budget is needed to achieve your target.

● Challenge the sponsor to get more funding.

● Recruit really motivated people.

Janine
- Hold a meeting very early in the project, to discuss the potential for conflict.
- Have open and honest feedback discussions every month.
- Discuss any issues before they turn into problems.

6 a a5 b4 c1 d2 e6 f3

B 2 *Suggested ideas for best-practice negotiation*
- Summarise your understanding of the other side's position/interests after it is explained.
- State your own interests/position (highlight where there is common interest).
- Check the other side understands your position/interests.
- Propose solutions.
- Reject unacceptable proposals politely.
- Bargain and offer compromises.
- Agree to a solution.
- Confirm and summarise the solution.
- Close positively.

3 a a project report and a final launch date to present to the sponsor
   b no time / busy collecting and analysing customer feedback
   c The sponsor is presenting the information to the board.
   d Two of Angela's best people have left the project.
   e He feels it is unacceptable.
   f He will speak to the sponsor.

5 a sign off b provide c agree d authorise
   e guarantee; hit f relocate

6 a2 b6 c4 d5 e1 f3

C 1 *Suggested answer*
E-mail can be a trigger for many reasons. The most problematic features of e-mail are that communication tends to be short and can be sent too fast without thinking. Poorly written e-mails can easily cause the reader to feel criticised and become offended.

2 *Suggested analysis*
Most readers would be quite critical of such an e-mail. It is brief and blunt. It seems to focus strongly on the negative (*mistakes*). Many people will also judge the statement at the end (*Please call me immediately*) as too direct, almost rude and disrespectful.

However, if we reflect more neutrally about this e-mail, we can see that Bob may have a positive motivation for writing. He is taking time to try and improve the quality of the presentation. He is being honest, saying what he thinks, because he believes this is the basis for a trusting relationship with his colleague. Interestingly, no part of the e-mail is explicitly critical of Julia, but simply describes the facts (*I found many mistakes*).

Finally, the statement at the end (*Please call me immediately*) is actually an invitation to further communication. And remember, we don't know Julia. She may be someone who responds positively to this form of communication, even if we don't. This exercise highlights the dangers of making negative judgements too quickly, something it is particularly easy to do when reading e-mails.

3 a It's more impersonal. People are not so close to the other person and the emotions of conflict.
   b We miss non-verbal information, which helps us to interpret the real emotions behind a message.
   c When we are unsure of how to interpret the emotions of others, we assume the worst and believe that someone has a negative reason for writing.
   d Before you reply to what you see as a negative e-mail. This helps to make sure your reply is professional and not too emotional.
   e Be careful, as it can look as if you are criticising people in front of their managers.
   f to set up a call or meeting to actually deal with the problem

5 *Suggested answers*
   a I hope you b thanks c writing d help/enable
   e really f questions/queries g wonder
   h you think i opinion/view j need
   k appreciate/realise/know l hesitate m best

D 1 a *Suggested answers*
   A Where I work, the teams are small and the roles are quite well defined. We have clear reporting lines to the team leader. It's not very hierarchical, so the team and the leader work quite closely together. Communication is open, and decision-making is done together.
   B It is quite a formal hierarchy. But our leaders have large areas of responsibility, so communication with them is not very regular. As they are some distance from our everyday work, we have the freedom to get on and make our own decisions.
   C We have a very informal structure in our team. Our boss is really like another colleague, someone we share ideas and questions with. We don't rely on her to make all the decisions, but her advice is always helpful.

2 **team roles**: Not defined so strongly, roles overlap, people give each other ideas for their part of the project
   leadership: The leader has a formal role, but is in the middle rather than above the team. The expectation is that team members share the leadership role.
   culture: The team culture is defined with a set of rules, particularly saying what is unacceptable (helps to integrate new team members quickly)
   conflict: Defining team rules / Discussing how to work together helps to avoid unnecessary conflict and misunderstanding

Case study commentary

1 There are different ways to read this e-mail. Firstly, it is easy to criticise it on many levels. The motivation of the e-mail is unclear, so it has the potential to be read as an attack. There is a risk that it looks like interference; Maria is advising, a role which Andrew may not accept, given that Maria is not his boss in any sense.

An alternative reading is to see the e-mail as some friendly advice. Maria has actually helped Andrew by re-motivating Kaneko and putting him back on track to deliver his project tasks. She is rightly keeping an eye on a friend in the organisation, showing concern for her friend. She actually provides Andrew with the useful information that Kaneko is overloaded with work, something of which Andrew may not be aware. And, in fact, her language in the e-mail is not actually critical, although it is somewhat direct in tone.

The e-mail touches on several important issues:

- How to influence something in a project (Kaneko's motivation) for which you, strictly speaking, have no formal responsibility. You may be seen as stepping into someone else's territory, which can lead to conflict.
- How to write clear e-mails, which others will read constructively. Maria's e-mail fails to do this.
- How to ensure that we do not react too quickly or too negatively to e-mails, assuming (perhaps wrongly) that the mail is blaming or attacking us.
- The need to build close relationships with colleagues so that when challenges do arise in a project, you have the necessary levels of mutual understanding and trust to resolve any potential problems constructively. It appears that Maria and Andrew have not yet managed to do this – a major failing of many who are working in international project teams.

There is no 'correct' answer to the e-mail. Perhaps the most low-risk solution would be for Maria to write as below. Her suggestion would then ensure the problem is discussed in a positive and open way.

Dear Andrew

I hope you are well. I hear that your part of the project is going well at the moment, which is great news for everyone involved.

I wonder if we could arrange a telephone call for next week. There are one or two things I would like to discuss with you and get your thoughts about. I am free all Monday and Tuesday afternoon, so just let me know a convenient time and I can give you a call.

Look forward to talking.

Best regards

Maria

2

Maria

Kaneko and I are working just fine, and our work is on target. When I need your advice, I'll be sure to ask for it. I really think it's better if you concentrate on your side of the project. Your e-mail isn't very helpful.

Sincerely,

Andrew

---

7 Marketing the project

A 1 a creating a name and a slogan
   b Effective marketing gets the engagement and support of people inside the organisation.
   c failure of the project

2 *Suggested answer*
   For small and medium-sized projects, progress reports and meetings may be all that is required in terms of communication. However, on a large project, all communication should take place within the context of an overall communications plan. Typically, marketing communication is used to build excitement and interest in a project. If there is a problem or change required in the project, it is much easier to implement a solution when the people involved are fully supportive of the project, rather than when they are confused, frightened or ambivalent. Especially if the project is controversial, the positive aspects of marketing communication become more and more critical.

3 a 10%
   b There was a lot of bad feeling.
   c The name 'Future business model' was given to the project, and intranet pages with basic information were created.
   d Not very. The communication challenge was underestimated.

4 b Asked the CEO to do a web interview; publicised all the company was doing to support staff who were affected; project leader devoted plenty of time to listening and explaining what was happening

5 a launch **b** announce **c** build **d** accomplish
   e represents **f** give **g** publish **h** link **i** copy
   j amend **k** update **l** approve **m** livening
   n prepare

6

verb	noun
announce	announcement
advertise	advertising / advertisement
accomplish	accomplishment
demonstrate	demonstration
publish	publication/publishing/publisher
amend	amendment
confirm	confirmation
approve	approval

B 1 a It should contain enough information in these areas to convince the listener to find out more about:
   - what the project is
   - what its key benefits are
   - who you are and why your project will be successful,

2 **Overall aim of the project:** to improve customer service
   Why the project is needed: research shows the company is behind the competition

Specific benefits the project will deliver: the website will makes progress chasing simpler and more convenient for general customers; key customers will receive better service because staff will have more time with them

Success story from the project so far: trial in Italy – 100% positive feedback

4 **a** plan to **b** achieve **c** bring in **d** ensure that we **e** enhance **f** minimise **g** align **h** slash **i** grow

6 **a** 5 **b** 4 **c** 6 **d** 2 **e** 7 **f** 3 **g** 1

C 3 1 g 2 d 3 e 4 b 5 c 6 a 7 f

4 **a** The case for change must contain hard facts and figures, so people really know what the change means and that it makes sense.

  b It can develop the self-belief for people to learn new skills.

  c Be honest and show a genuine interest in the greater good of the organisation.

  d That change can affect people's sense of their own ability, and therefore give rise to strong resistance.

  e Because some objections can lead to genuine improvements in the proposed idea.

6 **a** A number of complaints have been received that the project is generating high levels of stress in the team.

  b Many people suspect that management is using the project to make people redundant.

  c I'm concerned that the project will not deliver tangible benefits to the organisation.

  d Very few people believe that the project can be successful, because it doesn't have the necessary budget.

  e There's a lot of resistance to the new software from those who believe it's far too complex.

  f The project has received a lot of criticism, because implementation has been so slow over the last six months.

  g Users were very upset that they were not invited to participate during the design phase at the very beginning of the project.

D 1 a sales and marketing **b** IT/finance

2 Each department not only has its own ways of working, but also its own targets and priorities. This can lead to serious problems when co-operating, e.g. different views about what is important, how something should be done, when something should be done, etc.

3 **a a** She says there is customer demand and a gap in the market.

  b She says the proposed schedule is too short. Testing and approval may take longer due to new legal requirements.

  c He thinks the project has insufficient budget for expensive new packaging. He also has a lot of other projects to manage.

4 **b** Dmitry does not try to convince people of his arguments. He aims to convince people to co-operate. He does this by listening to what they have to say. He accepts that they have a point of view (Marie with her legal argument, Javier with the packaging cost and priorities issue) and suggests further discussion of their concerns at later meetings. With Javier, he suggests involving senior management if together they cannot solve the problem of conflicting priorities. We cannot yet say he is successful, but he has established agreement to move the project forward.

Case study commentary

Applying cultural intelligence to this case means *not* drawing too many conclusions from too little evidence. When working across cultures, it is extremely important to be able to suspend judgement and ask questions to find out what is really happening. This is possibly one of the most important intercultural competencies.

a Issues

1 The team seems to have an issue with how efficiently it develops ideas and proposals into concrete initiatives. However, we do not know how inefficient it is. The UK team has developed at least one design which has failed to prove effective.

2 Rashid's point of view is critical of his UK colleagues. He is judging the current team's behaviour on the basis of past (negative) experiences. This may possibly be clouding his judgement.

3 Rashid may have a valid point that the UK team's dominance is leading to imbalance and inefficiency in the project. There may be cultural and linguistic aspects involved (native vs. non-native speaker). The dominant style of behaviour may be unconscious or unintentional.

4 Rashid's decision to give such direct feedback on such a sensitive subject is questionable. The reaction of the UK team is not unexpected. Few would react positively to such criticism made in public in front of a project leader. Rashid should perhaps have consulted the project leader before the meeting.

b The project leader's authority in all of this is questionable. She is unaware of the strong undercurrents of negative feeling, suggesting she has not dedicated enough time to the team. Her decision to postpone the discussion to a teleconference, whilst practically motivated, is questionable, as this medium is also not ideally suited to conflict resolution.

c Various next steps are possible. Many would recommend one-to-one discussions between the project leader and the different parties (assuming the leader has credibility and skills to manage this). This allows people to express their views and for the leader to assess the level and nature of the conflict. A second step would be to set up a face-to-face workshop, focused on developing team performance and giving constructive feedback to each other. Within this process Eila would need to confirm a number of key messages:

  ● the need to co-operate positively and professionally as an international team

  ● the need to listen and respect other's points of view

  ● the idea that different points of view and different ways of working are of value for international

project teams, but challenging to manage sometimes
● the need to find a solution to the current situation urgently and move forward positively together

8 Finishing successfully

A 1 *Suggested answer*
A project is seen as 100% complete when all work-plan activities are complete and deliverables are approved by the project sponsor.
The project leader should:
1 Confirm in writing with the project sponsor that the project is complete.
2 Ensure all paperwork, agreements and supplier contracts are complete.
3 Conduct a 'lessons learned' meeting with the project team.
4 Hand over the project to an operations or support group.
5 Arrange for an appropriate celebration of the job done, to ensure that the project team feels appreciated.

2 *Suggested answer*
For individual team members, it is important to find time to reflect alone and then to discuss with the project leader and define steps for ongoing personal development.

3

	main success	main mistake	consequence of mistake
1	opened stores on time	no time to pass on what was learned from the project to others in the organisation	people making the same mistakes / wasted money
2	achieved a blend of the corporate brand and local design features	relied too much on video conferencing	made collaboration difficult in the first few months
3	have good sales	thinking more about the stores than sales training for staff	asking people to do training courses while they're busy

4 a/b

	alternative action	benefit
1	organise workshops after the project to capture lessons learned and publish it on intranet	would help leaders running similar projects in future
2	create a travel budget at the start of the project – to bring people together	more creative work and faster progress
3	start recruitment and training of sales staff at the beginning of the project	well-qualified staff when stores opened

6 a failures **b** blame **c** issue **d** underestimated **e** error **f** wrong **g** defect **h** fault **i** omitted **j** overlooked

7 *Suggested answers*
a If we had planned more carefully, we wouldn't have missed the deadlines. Our schedule should have been more realistic.
b If we had assessed the team's English, we wouldn't have had so many communication problems in meetings. We should have prioritised communication.
c If we had involved the sponsor, the project would have been easier to market. He should have been more available.
d If the team had dedicated the time, we could have delivered the right quality. Team members should have prioritised this project.
e If we'd had clear responsibilities, the key tasks would have been done. We should have clarified roles at the start of the project.

B 3 a a Training delivery has been outsourced.
b identifying the right supplier with the right quality levels
c the cost of bringing in two additional people
d no time to implement next year's online training catalogue
e Project leader offers to support people from IT to get the job completed.
b The sponsor should react positively to the news that the training has been successfully outsourced to a quality provider. However, the fact that the online training catalogue has not been implemented, and that the project leader can only support the implementation by others, may be seen as unsatisfactory. Questions may be asked to find out why the catalogue was not implemented and how much time the leader will actually have to support the work.

4 a Question 1: Why was the training catalogue delayed?
Answer: IT changes made this difficult.
Question 2: How soon will the catalogue be available?
Answer: By the middle or end of next month
Question 3: Can the training provider create the catalogue?
Answer: Good idea – but may be cost implications / something to discuss
Question 4: Should they postpone closing the project, as targets not reached?
Answer: Disagrees. Targets have been reached. Catalogue implementation was not in project scope.

5 a a I am delighted to confirm that all the major targets of the project have been achieved.
b I would like to take this opportunity to acknowledge the hard work of all the team.
c I think that there are probably only or two remaining issues to discuss.
d I am very confident that we can solve any outstanding issues quickly.

    e My recommendation would be for me to support the implementation for a couple of months.

    f I would like to express my appreciation for the support of the sponsor throughout this project.

6 a a5 b4 c3 d1 e7 f6 g8 h2

C 2 a They have to convince their clients that they have solid project management skills, which will guarantee they can deliver solutions for clients' business needs over time.

    b Salespeople signed contracts with clients which were often too demanding for project managers to deliver, either in terms of budgets or deadlines.

    c Many may lack understanding of the project technology, so making it difficult for them to understand decisions and provide leadership.

    d Key decisions on the project may be influenced by local management politics, culture or even religious beliefs.

    e It is an agreement between all those involved as to what constitutes success on a project. The project leader ultimately has responsibility to negotiate this.

    f It is important to enable them to respond to inevitable changes across organisations, which can make previous project planning out of date.

4 a halve **b** reinvent **c** rationalise **d** reduce **e** rethink **f** revamping **g** revised **h** reverse

D 3 a to identify some skill areas to improve for the next project

    b She is well organised and focuses on quality.

    c To understand that others might see your 'strengths' as a weakness. It's very important to understand how others see us.

    d People sometimes thought Julia was too inflexible. She didn't always address problems the rest of the team had, e.g. with resourcing.

4 a When pushing the team for results, Julia will take more time to explain her point of view and to listen more.

    b He asks how Julia is going to make sure she carries out her action plan.

    c Because it's helpful to be reminded of good practice.

Case study commentary

We do not have all the facts of the case, so it is very difficult to understand exactly what is happening here. It is clear that some people in the team have negative feelings about Helena's e-mail. This could be for many different reasons:

- Channel: Some people may not believe that it is appropriate to provide such feedback in an e-mail. They may expect a telephone call and may feel offended by the lack of personal contact.
- Style: The e-mail may be too short and neutral in tone for some people. They may judge the lack of emotion in the message as meaning that the message is not sincere.
- Culture: In some cultures, no feedback (saying nothing) is a sign that people have done a good job. It was expected that a good job would be done. The only feedback required would be negative – if the team hadn't met its objectives. Positive feedback of the type used by Helena could create the feeling: 'Why are you giving me this feedback? Are you surprised? Didn't you trust me to do my job?'
- Persons addressed: The e-mail was only sent to team members. Some may feel that feedback of this kind should be sent to management, in order to properly represent the team members' performance. Otherwise, some may feel it is meaningless.
- Expectation of reward: Some people are more motivated by bonuses than warm words, and it may be that this recognition by Helena is seen as a cheap form of rewarding the team.

There may be other factors involved. Depending on her sense of the importance of maintaining a relationship with the team members, Helena should probably meet or call each team member. Meeting with David will give her useful information as to her next steps.

Word list

International Management English

International Management English consists of four titles covering key aspects of international business operations: *Leading People*, *Managing Projects*, *Managing Change* and *Working Virtually*. These four titles provide insights into the challenges of working internationally and develop practical skills which will help people to do their jobs more effectively.

Each book in the series consists of eight units, with every unit offering four distinct sections:

- *Discussion and listening* Engaging and relevant content in areas of international management and teamwork.
- *Communication skills* In addition to the familiar topics of meetings, presentations and negotiations, input and practice are also provided in conflict management, team building and giving and receiving feedback.
- *Professional skills* Authentic texts from management writers and thinkers provide the starting point for reflection and discussion among learners.
- *Intercultural competence* A focus on raising cultural awareness followed by an illustrative case study.

Leading People
by Steve Flinders

This helps new and experienced managers to develop leadership skills for working and communicating internationally.

ISBN 978-1-905085-67-5

Managing Projects
by Bob Dignen

This provides practical ideas on how to work and communicate effectively when taking part in or leading international projects.

ISBN 978-1-905085-66-8

Managing Change
by Fiona Mee

This focuses on the communication requirements of those either taking part in or leading business change, including how to handle resistance.

ISBN 978-1-905085-68-2

Working Virtually
by Jackie Black and Jon Dyson

This addresses the communication challenges that global teams face when using information technology to collaborate.

ISBN 978-1-905085-69-9

For full details of this series, please visit the Delta Publishing website:
www.deltapublishing.co.uk